GRAPHIC ILLUSTRATION

IN

BLACK

AND

WHITE

GRAPHIC ILLUSTRATION

IN

BLACK

AND

WHITE

JACQUELINE GIKOW

DESIGN PRESS

First Edition
First Printing

Copyright © 1991 by Jacqueline Gikow

Printed in the United States of America

Designed by Beth Tondreau Design

Reproduction or republication of the content in any manner, without
the express written permission of the publisher, is prohibited. The
publisher takes no responsibility for the use of any of the materials
or methods described in this book, or for the products thereof.

Gikow, Jacqueline. 1947-
    Graphic illustration in black and white / Jacqueline Gikow.
      p. cm.
    ISBN 0-8306-9007-7
    1. Graphic arts. I. Title.
  NC845.G55   1990   90-3299
  741.6—dc20   CIP

Design Press offers posters and The Cropper, a device for cropping
artwork, for sale. For information, contact Mail-order Department.
Design Press books are available at special discounts for bulk
purchases, for sale promotions, fund raisers, or premiums. For details
contact Special Sales Manager.

Questions regarding the content of the book should be addressed to:

  Design Press
  11 West 19th Street
  New York, NY 10011

Design Press books are published by Design Press, an imprint of TAB
BOOKS. TAB BOOKS is a Division of McGraw-Hill, Inc. The Design
Press logo is a trademark of TAB BOOKS.

Any work not credited was done by the author.

ACKNOWLEDGMENTS

f I had known what would be involved in writing this book before I started, I am not sure that I would have begun. Now that it is over, however, I can say it was a wonderful and terrible experience that has left me enriched and enthusiastic. I am grateful to many people who helped make this book happen but will single out only a few here:

Joseph Shannon, Professor of Art at Trenton State College, for encouraging me to begin this project and for his helpful suggestions.

Mary Kennan, for her continued interest in this idea and for passing my proposal on to Design Press.

Nancy Green, editorial director at Design Press, for her advice, counsel, and humor.

Faith Hamlin, my agent, for her optimism.

All the illustrators whose work appears in these pages, for their generosity in sharing their thoughts and work. Their names, with reference to their work, appear in the index at the end of this book. Special thanks to Elaine Hodges, Ruth Lozner, and Steve Oles for sharing their book-writing experiences with me.

Trenton State College and all the students whose work appears in this text.

My friends, for their support and good wishes during the past year and a half.

CONTENTS

INTRODUCTION

B lack-and-white illustrations consti-
tute approximately 60 percent of the
commercial illustration in the over
32,000 periodicals published in the
United States. The thousands of illustrations that appear in the pages of
magazines and newspapers have become so common-
place that most people tend to take them for granted.
Little thought is given to the work involved in producing visual enhancement to what is largely throwaway
reading matter. But that lack of consideration says nothing about the value of illustrations—or their creators.
People often take for granted that which makes their
lives easier or more pleasant. That black-and-white
illustrations are generally unremarkable to the average
person proves that the field remains alive and well; their
prevalence makes them ordinary, even when their artistic merit is extraordinary. This book targets the vast
opportunities open to illustrators focusing on a black-
and-white, or monochromatic, approach (figs. I-1, I-2, I-
3).

Power Serve, an illustration for a review of a book on women's resources in
Philadelphia. Medium: Pen-and-ink. (Illustrator: Jacqueline Gikow)

Figure I-1. *With Sincere Depreciation*. Illustration for an article in a computer software magazine. The editor wanted the illustration to enhance dry technical copy, and so the illustrator used images of magic to attract the reader. Medium: Pencil. (Illustrator: Kathleen Volp)

Figure I-2. *Happy Valentine's Day*. Illustration for a greeting card. Medium: Pen-and-ink. (Illustrator: Jacqueline Gikow)

Figure I-3. Portrait of Frank Lloyd Wright, used to publicize collectible postage stamps. Media: Pen-and-ink, gouache. (Illustrator: Kevin Sprouls; © *Reader's Digest*)

Illustration is from the Latin *lustrare*, meaning "to make bright," and that indeed is what such an image does for a text. Its main purpose is to clarify, to explain a concept more effectively and efficiently. At its most straightforward, an illustration provides information, as in a map or how-to diagram. At its most complex, an illustration interprets or comments on the material it accompanies. Whether dramatizing a story or selling a product, arousing curiosity or emphasizing a message, providing entertainment or provoking thought, an illustration succeeds or fails based on its ability to communicate with the viewer (fig. I-5).

Not every illustration is a drawing, and not every drawing is an illustration. Graphs, charts, paintings, collages, and photographs, as well as drawings, may all be used to clarify a text. Conversely, some drawings are intended to stand alone, be they doodles or works of art, without meaning related to accompanying text or objects. Both illustration and drawing provide means of solving problems, interpreting concepts, communicating in aesthetically pleasing and visually stimulating ways.

Although you may use other methods to create your final image, an ability to draw well will enable you to develop illustration ideas quickly and effectively. Drawing from life is one of the best ways to learn how to look and to analyze the way you see. Understanding why the world looks as it does makes you better able to imagine alternatives. Meanwhile, achieving proficiency through practice, mastering the basics of anatomy and perspective, provides a firm foundation for your work as an illustrator. A list of general drawing books can be found in the bibliography.

Since the development of the camera, art directors, advertisers, and publishers, as well as photographers and illustrators, have debated the merits of the mechanically captured image versus that created by hand. During the last hundred years, photography has largely replaced illustration for factual documentation, while the intangible areas of fantasy, fiction, editorial, advertising, and technical innovation have developed as new horizons for illustration. The artist can often illustrate what the camera cannot show.

Most art buyers consider the requirements of an individual assignment before deciding whether to commission photography or illustration. In many cases, of course, the budget sets the limitations. This works in the favor of illustrators, since their work tends to be the less costly choice.

This book assumes a basic proficiency in drawing and will not be of much use to those who cannot draw at all. Although it provides instructions for specific media and techniques, the book aims at helping beginning and professional illustrators learn how to stand out in a competitive field.

You will find examples from illustrators working exclusively or partially in black-and-white media, using varied techniques, displaying individual styles, and addressing many different markets. Where possible, the contributors have provided information on how their style or technique was adapted for an assignment. As the book progresses, it explains and demystifies the creative process as well as the business side of graphic illustration.

Chapters 1 and 2 concentrate on developing an approach to an assignment. Chapters 3 through 6 describe specific media and techniques (fig. I-6). Chapter 7 discusses specialized markets (fig. I-7), while chapter 8 concentrates on issues of content and developing a distinctive style (fig. I-8). Finally, chapter 9 shows you how to put it all together in a professional style.

You can use the book as a self-instruction guide or classroom text. It includes exercises along with suggested portfolio projects. Beginning, intermediate, or advanced students can cover all of the material in one or two semesters.

Figure I-4. Fashion illustration for self-promotion. Media: Charcoal, pastel, and stamp lettering. (Illustrator: Thea Kliros)

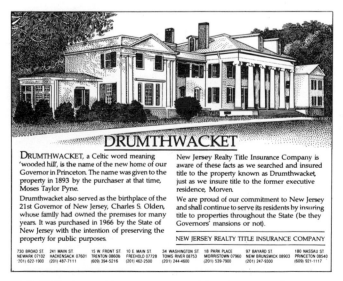

Figure I-5. Real estate insurance company ad for a law journal. The illustration is intended to instill confidence and convey substance. Medium: Pen-and-ink. (Illustrator/designer: Kevin Sprouls; copy: W. A. Sprouls)

Figure I-7. Fashion illustration in silhouette style, used as part of a poster for a shopping mall. Media: Cut Pantone film on multimedia vellum. (Illustrator: Elvira Regine)

Figure I-6. Illustration of a house commissioned by a private client. The drawing uses a variety of lines to create rich patterns and textures. Medium: Pen-and-ink. (Illustrator: Anne Weisz)

Figure I-8. *Now You See It* . . . . For a magazine article reviewing new computer software, this illustration uses symbolism from a magic show. Medium: Pen-and-ink. (Illustrator: Jacqueline Gikow)

CHAPTER 1

THE ILLUSTRATION PROCESS

Every illustration assignment has specific requirements and individual limitations. That these change from client to client, from assignment to assignment, makes an illustrator's work interesting and occasionally frustrating. In general, illustration assignments have three characteristics: a subject, including any written material, such as a text or a slogan, that the illustration will accompany; a set of dimensions, or format; and a schedule, or time frame.

Subject. To do the best possible job, your first step will be to become familiar with your assignment by reviewing the material you are given. If a subject is unfamiliar, you might do some research or find out from your client if additional resource material is available. Assignments range from simple to complex, straightforward to interpretive; many, of course, fall somewhere between these extremes. For a straightforward assignment, the client

Night Fishing, an illustration for the outdoors column of a newspaper describing the highs and lows of fishing at night. Media: Ink, white gouache on illustration board. (Illustrator: Glenn Wolff)

provides a specific subject, such as "a hammer" or "hand displaying a ring" (fig. 1-1). In advertising, a precise layout for each element is often included. All that is required of the illustrator is a skilled rendering of the subject without changes in design or imagery (which, however creative, will not be welcome). For an interpretive illustration, on the other hand, you might be given a manuscript, plot synopsis, or ad copy line to illustrate, with the freedom to choose the imagery and no instructions as to conceptual approach (figs. 1-2, 1-3).

Format. For any assignment the client stipulates the final format of the illustration, which may be given as a general dimension (square, vertical, horizontal) or as a specific set of measurements. Sometimes ratios are used to indicate relative height and width; for example, a

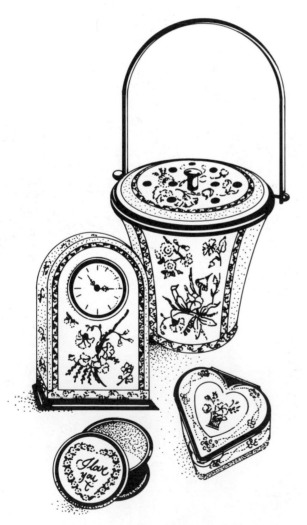

Figure 1-1. Illustration of a selection of giftware, used in a newspaper ad. The client, a florist, requested a drawing that showed the intricate decorative patterns on the items. Media: Rapidograph on vellum. (Illustrator: Laura Hutton)

Figure 1-2. For the same client who commissioned figure 1-1, this illustration employs a more interpretive approach. Both flowers and giftware are represented, but the setting is both imaginative and humorous. Media: Rapidograph on vellum. (Illustrator: Laura Hutton)

Figure. 1-3. *Author Lee Gutkind Pauses for a Rest*, for a book on backwoods people of Pennsylvania. The artist was given a free rein to develop images to accompany the text. Reference material was obtained by visiting various sites mentioned in the book and taking Polaroid pictures for reference back in the studio. Media: Graphite and watercolor dyes on Strathmore three-ply board. (Illustrator: Frederick H. Carlson)

three-to-one vertical format would mean the drawing may be any size, provided its height is three times its width. Often illustrations are executed larger than they will be when printed, and general dimensions are sufficient as long as you work in the correct proportions. Measurements may include allowances for bleed if the illustration extends to the trimmed edge of the page on one, two, three, or all four sides.

Time Frame. The average time given to complete an illustration is two weeks. (More complex assignments, such as a corporate annual report or a book, may require as much as a month or two, while newspaper deadlines often fall within twenty-four hours.) Typically, the first week consists of research, design, and concept presentation. The next day or so is used for approval and revision, and the rest of the schedule is allotted for execution of the finished piece. The assignment deadline is the date your illustration is due. If you are unreliable in meeting deadlines, you will almost surely find yourself with a very short and unprofitable career (fig. 1-4).

STAGES OF THE ILLUSTRATION

Whatever its function, an illustration must communicate with impact, and so you must explore a variety of alternative approaches to any assignment to present the most effective one. Sometimes you plan an illustration around structured visual ideas already selected to match written copy; other times the illustration evolves as you experiment. The creative stages of the visual design process of an illustration include thumbnails, roughs, and final presentation (figs. 1-5, 1-6, 1-7).

Thumbnails. Once you have completed the research and are familiar with your subject, begin to make small idea sketches, called thumbnails. Drawn in proportion

Figure 1-4. *Country/City Gardening*, for a newspaper article on the similarites and differences of gardening in the city and country. A tight deadline required a quick start, so the artist and art director (who was familiar with the artist's style) discussed the concept—a two-panel approach—on the phone. The camera-ready art was delivered the following day. The artist did a comprehensive sketch to transfer onto white scratchboard using graphite paper but did not have to show the sketch to the art director. Media: Scratchboard and india ink. (Illustrator: Ruth Lozner)

Figure 1-5. The illustrator examined a variety of ways of depicting the subject on a sketchbook page and then called the art director to discuss the concepts.

Figure 1-6. After selecting a concept, the artist proceeded to a rough pencil drawing for transfer to a linoleum block.

Figure 1-7. *Child Support Laws*, for an article in the *Boston Globe* on the Massachusetts child-support program. Medium: Linoleum block print. (Illustrator: David Street; art director: Jane Simon)

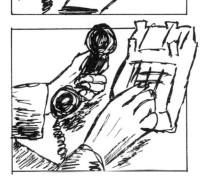

Figure 1-8. The thumbnail sketches for the illustration in figure 1-9 show the variety of approaches possible even when the subject is limited. The author requested a very straightforward approach to a set of instructions on phoning for assistance.

Figure 1-9. Illustration of a hand dialing a phone, from an instructional text on job hunting, geared toward people without high school degrees. Medium: Pen-and-ink. (Illustrator: Douglas Reinke; publisher: Peterson's) .

to the dimensions of the finished piece but measuring one-quarter of its size, these sketches should be quick and relatively undetailed, to facilitate idea generation. Fill a sheet of paper (tracing paper and lightweight bond are excellent) with miniature outlines of the desired format, then complete each with a different idea. Think about your subject, freely associate, and without making value judgments, sketch every idea you have about the topic. If your subject is straightforward, like the telephone in figure 1-9, for example, you can still play with detail, textures, and subtle composition changes (fig. 1-8). If your subject must be interpreted, you have many more choices (figs. 1-10, 1-11, 1-12). Try each idea from many angles, high and low as well as close-up and distant views. Then draw a few variations of one or two good ideas. You may want to cut and paste or combine images by tracing to achieve different effects.

Seasoned illustrators recognize the value of the thumbnail stage of design: the more you develop your ideas through these preliminary sketches, the stronger the choices for your final illustration will be. Such experimentation strengthens the final solution. Indeed,

Figure 1-10. The art director requested an illustration for a poster for a jazz festival in a southern seaside resort using a combination of images reflecting the music genre and the beach environment. The artist presented six rough concepts that ranged from figurative to graphic. (Illustrator: Bill Mayer)

Figure 1-11. The client chose the most graphic approach (the fan combines the seashell with piano keys), and the artist developed a number of approaches for the poster designs. (Illustration: Bill Mayer)

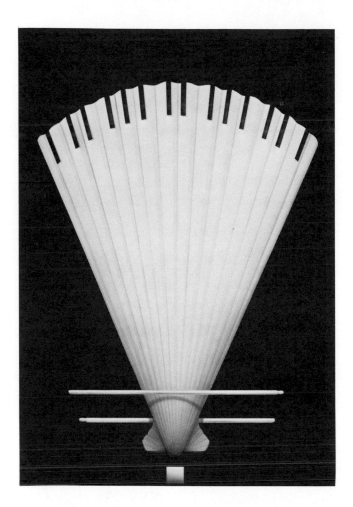

Figure 1-12. Poster for the Spoleto Jazz Festival. The poster was commissioned in black-and-white instead of full color, not because of cost economies but because the art director felt the result would be more elegant. Media: Airbrush dyes, gouache. (Illustrator: Bill Mayer)

for a beginner or a student, thumbnails are often more important than the final project, because they demonstrate the thought, creativity, and experimentation that bring about solutions. Keep all of your thumbnails. You may find some of the ideas useful later, and prospective employers may wish to see evidence of your imagination and discipline.

Roughs. Once you have fully explored a range of ideas in thumbnails, select the best two or three for refinement. The purpose of the preliminary rough is to test ideas on a larger scale and to work out problems that could not be foreseen or resolved at the thumbnail stage. As you progress from the thumbnail to the rough sketch, redefining and rethinking, you may find that your memory provides insufficient detail to draw upon, and that you need additional visual aids such as still-life props or photographs (see chapter 2).

Illustration assignments almost always require you to submit a rough drawing for approval so that the client can get an idea of the finished product. At this stage you make changes to suit your client's needs, and sometimes you must provide two or more rough drawings for the client to review. Execute your presentation rough in the same shape and proportions required for the final product, the same size specified for the reproduction or slightly larger, but no more than twice the finished size. Render them neatly in pencil or ink, but without adding time-consuming textures or intricate details (figs. 1-13, 1-14).

Finished Artwork. Once the client has approved the rough drawing and perhaps indicated changes on it, you may proceed to the finished illustration. If the changes are substantial, the client may want to see another rough; otherwise your final contact with the client will be delivery of the completed artwork. Make minor alterations directly on the rough; if the changes are extensive, develop a new drawing to incorporate them. This drawing should be the same size as the finished artwork will be so that you can transfer your layout to the appropriate rendering surface.

Preparing final art approximately one-and-a-half times the reproduction size is standard practice. This enlargement makes it easier to draw detail; this may be especially helpful when doing tight, realistic work such as product illustration or some genres of editorial illustration (fig. 1-15). Later, photographic reduction will sharpen lines and make edges look more precise. If you are using a looser, painterly, gestural style, however, it may be more appropriate to work at a smaller scale or at the same size as the finished reproduction.

Always submit illustrations with crop marks indicating the functional illustration area. Crop marks are fine lines, usually made with a technical pen, placed at the boundaries of the image to help in the scaling of the illustration during production (fig. 1-16). Especially important on illustrations that have bleeds or those that float on the page without a border, crop marks enable the production people to scale your work and to place it in the proper position.

PRESENTATION

Presentation is an important part of the illustration process and a professional necessity, so do not short-change it. A properly packaged product makes a good impression on a client. Protecting your illustration shows that you care about your work, which makes that work more precious, increases the likelihood of its getting respectful consideration, and enhances your image as a professional (fig. 1-17).

After you complete an illustration, center-mount it on white illustration or mat board, leaving a two- or three-inch border. Attach the illustration to the board with either masking tape or white artist's tape, which

Figure 1-13. This rough sketch for one of twenty habitat illustrations for a book is shown completed in figure 1-14. After completing the roughs, the artist met with the author. The notes on the rough drawing were made during the discussions. The artist had free rein in design, style, and technique as long as landscape, anatomy, and placement of animals in insets and borders were correct. Media: 2B pencil on vellum. (Illustrator: Glenn Wolff)

Figure 1-14. *Appalachian Cove Forest* from *The Field Guide to Wildlife Habitats of the Eastern United States*, by Janine M. Benysus. Media: Technical pen on illustration board. (Illustrator: Glenn Wolff)

Figure 1-15. This self-promotional line illustration was executed in a fifteen-by thirty-inch format. This is an 80 percent reduction, which is much smaller than would normally be attempted. Medium: Pen-and-ink. (Illustrator: Chuck McVicker).

will not tear the drawing if removed or adjusted. Use a piece of tracing paper or acetate cut larger than the board for a protective overlay, and secure this at the top with a long strip of tape.

At this point the artwork is protected from handling while being viewed but is still vulnerable to damage in transit. (Remember that the artwork will travel at least to the client's office, to the production department, and back to the client before returning to you, so the package must be secure.) Cut a sheet of opaque paper larger than the art and slightly longer than the board. Tape this sheet to the top of the back of the mat board, and then bend it over to cover the entire board. Large sheets of inexpensive paper, called cover stock, are perfect for this purpose and are available in art supply stores.

Finally, use a sharp mat knife to trim all layers flush to the mount board. Attach your business card or a sticker with your name, address, and telephone number on it to the lower right-hand corner of the cover flap. Place the covered illustration in a manila envelope addressed to the client.

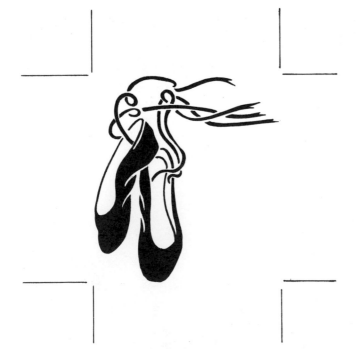

Figure 1-16. Crop marks on this illustration of ballet shoes, used on an invitation for a ballet benefit, helped the printer determine how much room the image required. Medium: Pen-and-ink. (Illustrator: Jacqueline Gikow)

EXERCISES

1. Choose a straightforward subject, such as a chair or a hand displaying a ring. Make three thumbnail sketches. Choose one thumbnail and create a rough drawing.

2. Choose a poem, short story, or other piece of fiction. Make six thumbnail sketches interpreting your choice. Develop one thumbnail into two rough drawings. Execute a finished illustration, eight inches wide by ten inches long.

3. Create an interpretive illustration for a nonfiction magazine article; the format is horizontal in a one-to-two ratio. Make six thumbnail sketches; then create a rough drawing for presentation.

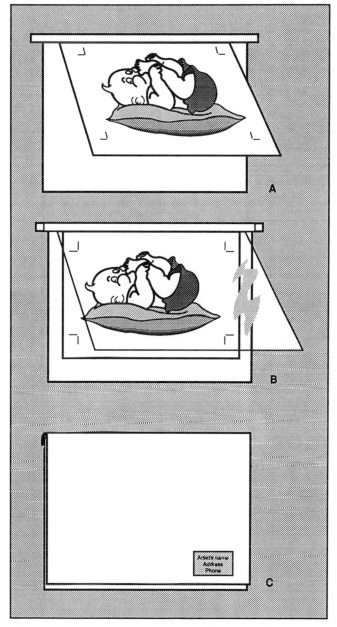

Figure 1-17. Protecting your illustration shows that you care about your work and lessens the likelihood of damage. (*A*) The illustration is mounted on a piece of white illustration or mat board, with a two- or three-inch border. (*B*) A piece of tracing paper or acetate cut larger than the board is used as a protective overlay. (*C*) A sheet of opaque paper covers the illustration and is taped to the top of the back of the mat board.

CHAPTER 2

SOURCE MATERIAL AND PROJECTION TECHNIQUES

America Beckons to Foreign Foods, for a newspaper article comparing imported food with American substitutions. The illustrator used a popular painting, *American Gothic*, by Grant Wood, as the primary source for this illustration. Food photos from magazines were also used, as was a library book on flags. Medium: Pen-and-ink. (Illustrator: Janice Belove)

hether your illustration is set in the modern world or an ancient one, drawn from life or from your imagination, you must depict its characters, objects, and scenery in a believable way, with details that convey a sense of time and place. Having the person, thing, or setting in front of you provides the most information about it, of course (fig. 2-1), but some subjects are simply inaccessible.

Few illustrators rely totally on memory and imagination. It is difficult to remember the exact appearance of things with which you are familiar, let alone represent people and places you have never known or visited. For this reason illustrators use visual references to aid them in creating and enriching their work, as well as ensuring its accuracy.

SOURCE FILE

Your client may provide reference material for an assignment (fig. 2-2). If not, or if you need additional

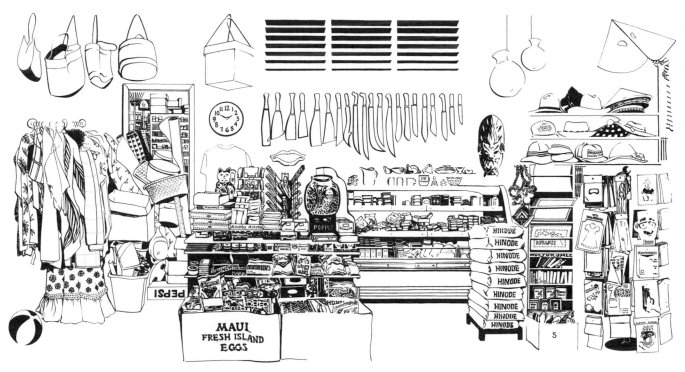

Figure 2-1. *The Hasegawa General Store*, drawn on-site, chosen by Small Business Hawaii to be used on its membership certificate. Medium: Crowquill pen and ink. (Illustrator: Ramsay)

Figure 2-2. Merchandise fixture illustration, used on a product promotion page for a manufacturer of store equipment. The client provided source material in the form of blueprint plans. Medium: Pen-and-ink. (Illustrator: Jacqueline Gikow)

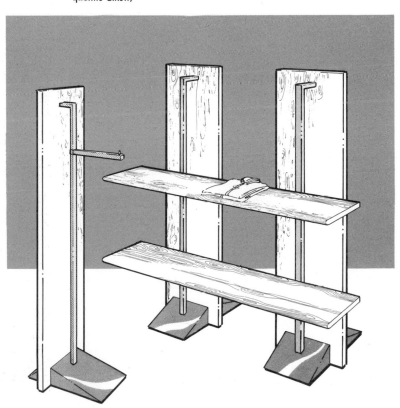

Figure 2-3. *Political Mail*, from an article on promoting candidates through the U.S. Postal Service. The illustrator used familiar images of national political mascots from magazines as reference for this illustration. Medium: Prismacolor on coquille board. (Illustrator: Janice Belove)

material, you can do research in a library or bookstore (fig. 2-3). Research can be time consuming, however, so many illustrators build source files containing pictures of various subjects. Such reference collections may contain, for example, magazine clippings, photographs, postcards, and mail-order catalogs. Other good sources of visual information include illustrated books, such as surveys of musical instruments or collections of birds, and pictorial encyclopedias filled with old engravings (figs. 2-4, 2-5). A number of publishers of copyright-free printed illustrations and designs, called clip art, offer subscription services. And if you have a computer with graphics capabilities, you might investigate the growing number of clip-art libraries on disk. In any case, the time you invest building a storehouse of reference material will pay off in a smoother, more rewarding creative process.

Collage illustrators often use their source material in the work itself. Cutting up source material to use in each piece can make short work of a reference file, however, and so they may photocopy or photostat it and return the original to its file (fig. 2-6).

A complete, up-to-date source file can take up quite a bit of room. As your collection expands, keeping it

Figure 2-4. Woodcut for *Solnemann der Unsichtbare*, by A. M. Frey, 1914. (Illustrator: Otto Nuckel; courtesy Delphin-Verlag, Munich)

Figure 2-5. *Hiring (and Keeping) Valuable WP Operators.* Illustration for a magazine article discussing the hiring practices for word-processing employees. The reference for this illustration was the woodcut in figure 2-4. Medium: Pen-and-ink. (Illustrator: Jacqueline Gikow)

Figure 2-6. *What Makes a Great Cook Great?* from a newspaper article exploring the differences between cooks who seem inspired and people who just like to cook. The illustration uses photocopied images from the artist's reference files. Medium: Paper collage with engravings. (Illustrator: Joan Hall)

organized is vital. Dedicate a file cabinet to this material or set up individual scrapbooks for each subject. The file headings you might use to classify your own collection include:

Human Figure: men, women, children, groups, feet, hands, heads, famous, executives, the elderly, fashion, exercise, sports

Architecture, Commercial and Industrial: buildings, cityscapes, churches, interiors, rural, schools

Architecture, Residential: contemporary, traditional, historic, kitchens, bathrooms, living spaces

Design: graphics, lettering, trademarks, charts, maps, rendering techniques

Fauna: mammals, birds, fish, insects, reptiles

Flora: gardens, houseplants, trees, shrubs, vegetables, fruits, flowers

Products, Commercial: heavy equipment, machines, tools

Products, Consumer: appliances, decorations, sporting equipment, furniture, cookware, tableware

Science: computer systems and hardware, medical facilities, laboratory equipment, space programs

Transportation: aircraft, ships and boats, cars and trucks, highways, trains

USING PHOTOGRAPHS

Drawing from a photograph is convenient because the person behind the camera has already done some of the work for you, namely transforming the subject into a two-dimensional image. When you use that image as a source of reference, however, it should enhance your imagination rather than replace it. If you reproduce an original image, you run the risk of infringing upon the copyright of your source. If you work directly from a photograph found in a book or magazine, for instance, you need to obtain permission from the image's copyright holder. Moreover, a photograph may not completely fulfill your illustration's requirements: it may have poor lighting, be taken from an improper angle, or supply the wrong mood or insufficient choice of viewpoints.

It is best not to become overly dependent on photo references. Use them in different ways. Copy parts of photographs and invent the rest; combine elements from different sources; employ a drawing style that alters the strict realism of the reference; change viewpoint, contrast, or even gender of the subject (figs. 2-7, 2-8). Take only what you need from sources to enhance your own ideas.

TAKING PHOTOGRAPHS

When you are unable to render a subject from life, it often is faster and easier to produce pictures for reference than to search for them. Sometimes you can instruct a company photographer to take the pictures you want. But taking your own photographs eliminates the need to compromise, and you can copy or trace them to the last detail. When you use the camera to create your own reference material, you control the angles, the lighting, and the position of the subject (figs. 2-9, 2-10). You can take any number of views—focusing on the central figure, background texture, or interesting

Figure 2-7. Three reference photographs used for figure 2-7. The client wanted to show three different sandwiches. As source material, the artist made each sandwich and photographed it. The references were then combined to develop the horizontal layout. (Photo: David McKelvey)

Figure 2-8. An illustration used in a newspaper advertisement for a bread company. The agency art directors wanted a crisp, clean illustration that would dependably reproduce on newsprint. Black-and-white food illustration is a challenge because food is recognizable by its color as well as shape. To illustrate food successfully, you must be able to render its texture as well as determine the right values. Media: Airbrush with transparent inks. (Illustrator: David McKelvey)

Figure 2-9. This photo reference was used to develop both figures for the illustration in figure 2-10. (Photo: Robert Herman)

details—to provide the raw material for interpretation. If your illustration calls for figures, set up scenes with friends or paid models. The camera allows you to capture varied and difficult poses in an instant.

Camera and Film Considerations. It is very easy to be sidetracked by the seductive world of photography, which may take away from the time and energy required to perfect your illustration skills. Consider your needs realistically to determine how involved with the technical side of photography you should become. Many illustrators use a Polaroid camera to create quick reference material. Simple to operate, it provides an immediate image, but its disadvantages include the small size of the print, poor control over the image area, and expensive film.

The 35mm single-lens-reflex camera requires some technical understanding, but its operation can be learned fairly quickly. Most 35mm cameras work both automatically and manually, giving you different degrees of control, and accept three types of film: slide, color print, and black-and-white print.

Some slide film can be processed within three hours, making it almost as convenient as Polaroid, which it surpasses in terms of image control and sharpness of detail. The problem with slides is that you need a projector to create an image of usable size. Some color-print film can also be processed quickly and inexpensively (in many cases only an hour is required). Quick-process printing limits you to a three- by five-inch format, adequate for source material as long as poor lighting does not diminish detail.

Easier to shoot and less sensitive to the light quality than color, black-and-white film requires more processing time. Black-and-white film allows freer interpretation of the image (without the distraction of color information) and can be printed inexpensively in a variety of sizes.

Photographic Distortion and Drawing. Do not assume that a photograph taken from life perfectly interprets it. In fact, the camera changes contours and perspective, and copying this distortion will weaken your illustration. Integrating a photographic reference into a composition calls for creativity as well as a basic understanding of the way lenses work.

Human eyes view objects from two different points: the field of vision in each eye overlaps. Both lenses focus sharply and continuously in fractions of a second, together producing a single, uniformly sharp impression of physical volume.

Figure 2-10. *Boku-Maru*, from an article on promoting enthusiasm in teaching literature, published in *Media & Methods*. The illustration draws on literary references in the article. Medium: Pen-and-ink. (Illustrator: Jacqueline Gikow)

Most cameras do the same work through a single lens. This results in an image flatter than one naturally perceived, which makes evaluating actual sizes and spatial relationships difficult. Depending upon the choice of lens, f-stop (the size of the lens opening, which determines how much light is allowed in when you take the photograph), exposure time, and distance, the camera captures only a limited depth of field with absolute sharpness. Every figure photographs somewhat shorter and thicker through the middle than it really is. When you see a photograph, your brain compensates for the distortion, reading perspective and foreshortening as correct; in the same way, your hand will have to make adjustments when rendering the image.

PROJECTING AND TRACING TECHNIQUES

After choosing reference materials, you must often transfer them to a form appropriate for your illustration assignment. This may mean tracing or projecting an image or part of one onto a drawing surface. You can also apply the techniques described here to tracing freehand drawings or to transferring a rough drawing onto the final rendering surface.

Tracing from a Slide Projector. A projector enlarges the image on a slide by projecting it onto a screen, wall, or board. The focal length, or the distance

Figure 2-11. Reference photos for figure 2-12. The artist often makes several reference photos, overexposed to bring out the details in darker areas and underexposed to retain the detail in the lighter areas. The reference was photographed outdoors to create well-defined shadows on the subject. (Photos: David McKelvey)

from the projector to the screen, will determine the size of the projected image. The greater the focal length, the larger the image. Tape your drawing paper to the projection surface at a height comfortable for drawing, and dim the lights: the darker the room, the clearer the image. Your paper should have a frame, lightly sketched in pencil, to the dimensions of the illustration. This enables you to judge projection size and to guide the image to the right location. Then sketch the image in outline, including as much detail as needed. When you complete the tracing and remove the projection, your drawing will be a maze of guidelines to be refined or stylized.

Tracing from an Opaque Projector. An opaque projector projects a reflective image—a photograph (not a slide), a reproduction from a book or magazine, a sketch—directly onto a drawing surface by an arrangement of mirrors. This device can enlarge an image up to three times its original size or reduce it by one-third. The size of the original that the projector will hold varies from model to model. Along with enlarging thumbnail and rough sketches, you can project portions of several sketches onto one surface.

Tracing with a Light Table. The principle behind a light table, basically a light bulb mounted under a glass plate and supported in a frame, is that it is easier to trace an image that is lit from behind. When you place a photo or drawing on the light table and cover it with drawing paper, light shining through the glass brightens the image and lights the paper to the point of transparency.

Light tables come in different sizes and styles. They allow you to trace material at the same size as the original. Portable light boxes that are small enough to sit on your drawing table are also available.

To construct a temporary light box, use a piece of glass (or Plexiglas) about eighteen by twenty-four inches in size. Frosted glass, which diffuses light evenly and prevents glare, is excellent, but clear glass will work as well. Cover the edges with masking tape to make them safe to handle. Balance the edges of the glass on top of two even stacks of books about five inches high, then place a small, flexible desk lamp underneath so that it shines up through the glass.

Tracing with Transfer Paper. Transfer paper is a thin sheet of paper with a layer of erasable powder on one side. When pressed it releases the powder, in the

Figure 2-12. Bowl of fruit used in a public-service newspaper ad for a hospital. Notice that the woven fruit basket used in the reference photo was changed to a wooden bowl for the final image. Media: Airbrush, gouache. (Illustrator: David McKelvey)

same way that carbon paper releases ink. Transfer paper comes in a number of colors, including graphite, nonreproducible blue, and white. It can be used to transfer source material onto a preliminary sketch or to transfer a rough to drawing paper or illustration board.

Place the transfer paper between the image to be traced and the paper to receive the tracing, with the coated side facing the blank paper. Test the degree of pressure needed to produce a guideline. Pressing too hard will produce a dark line that may be incised into the drawing surface and will be difficult to erase. Pressing too lightly results in an incomplete transfer of the image.

Photocopying. An important tool for the illustrator, the photocopier makes reproductions in pure black-and-white. You can use it to copy, enlarge, or reduce photographs, printed source material, and sketches inexpensively and quickly. Without harming the original drawing, you can transfer your work to a variety of papers, make changes, and test ideas. You can save time by enlarging or reducing a rough sketch to presentation size when you are ready to do the finished illustration. Photographs will lose their intermediary grays, but the copy should retain enough detail to provide a usable impression.

SILHOUETTES

Silhouette illustration for a utility company advertising the benefits of an energy-efficient home. The illustrator strove for believable gestures to create drama and used some flat pattern to add interest. Medium: Cut Amberlith. (Illustrator: Bill Mayer)

T he silhouette, also called a *profile* or *shadow illustration* is a two-dimensional, filled-in, usually one-color representation of the outline of a person, scene, or object. At its simplest the silhouette is nothing but the subject's profile, and there is a sharp distinction between its edge and the background. This ancient artform dates back to animal shadows drawn on the walls of prehistoric cave dwellings.

The word *silhouette* originated in eighteenth-century France and is attributed to Etienne de Silhouette, an amateur cutter of shadow portraits (profiles snipped out of paper with small, sharp scissors). By the early twentieth century, as the camera came into general use, the silhouette seemed a quaint, outdated means of portraiture.

In recent times, however, contemporary graphic designers have explored and expanded the possibilities of this versatile graphic device (figs. 3-1, 3-2, 3-3, 3-4). Although its technique has little in common with the

Figure 3-1. Logo design for an educational group organized by concerned parents. Medium: Pen-and-ink. (Designer/illustrator: Jacqueline Gikow)

Figures 3-2, 3-3, 3-4. Silhouettes of pregnant woman and babies from an article on resources for new mothers. Medium: Pen-and-ink. (Illustrator: Anne Weisz)

cut-paper shadow portraits of old, silhouette-based illustration produces similar results. It provides a distinctive alternative to modeled or realistic rendering. One of its benefits is universality; for example, the male and female figures on public rest-room doors and the basic shapes on traffic signs are easily understood silhouettes. The silhouette also seems uniquely suited to conveying elegance, humor, nostalgia, utility (figs. 3-5, 3-6).

Illustrators may combine the profile with other techniques (fig. 3-7) or concentrate on mastering that basic, necessarily exact line. Creating a silhouette depends entirely on a careful study of form: the subject's defining shapes, stripped of internal detail, must be dominant and well defined (fig. 3-8). Looking for silhouetted images is a good way to develop your awareness of the patterns created by the contrast of light and dark.

Figure 3-5. *Grass beyond the Mountains*. Silhouette of horses and rider from a book cover. Medium: Pen-and-ink. (Illustrator: Chuck McVicker)

Figure 3-6. Student silhouette illustration for an assignment to introduce humor into an interaction. Medium: Cut paper. (Illustrator: Stacey Rentel)

Figure 3-7. *Philadelphia Strut*, from a newspaper article on Philadelphia politics and job issues. Juxtaposing silhouettes of buildings, people, and a city street map creates a dancelike complexity that reflects the article's message. Medium: Pen-and-ink. (Illustrator: Jacqueline Gikow)

Figure 3-8. Student silhouette illustration showing a figure in action. Medium: Cut paper. (Illustrator: Student, name unknown)

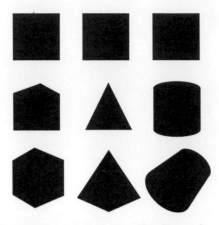

Figure 3-9. The three squares in the top row are ambiguous, because they do not suggest specific three-dimensional forms. The representations in the middle row begin to suggest distinct three-dimensional shapes. The three silhouettes in the bottom row clearly depict three-dimensional form: a cube, a cylinder, and a pyramid.

Figure 3-10. What appears to be a rectangular piece of paper is shown in varied positions from ground to horizon. Without further clues, the brain generally assumes that this is one flat form in a sequence of positions, rather than five different shapes. At eye level the rectangle appears as a straight line, while at ground level, you perceive depth through the silhouetted simulation of perspective. (Illustrator: Scott Pinkava)

EQUIPMENT

To draw or paint a silhouette, you will need a smooth, plate-finished bristol or illustration board, a pencil, a few brushes and a tube of opaque paint, or a pen and india ink. To cut a silhouette, you need a thin, opaque paper, a pencil, and an X-Acto knife with a supply of sharp no. 11 blades. You can also tear a silhouette from paper, assemble it as a collage, or print one using a variety of techniques.

CREATING THE SILHOUETTED FORM

Creation of a clear, unambiguous silhouette depends on finding the right viewpoint: one that communicates a sense of perspective and suggests the presence of a third dimension. By eliminating distracting details of form and color, you can concentrate attention on the shape of the subject and make its outline easier to "read." The viewer then recognizes form through certain visual clues that reflect missing pieces, calling upon common knowledge of form to complete the picture. Natural ability to see and comprehend a three-dimensional world operates even when the eye confronts a flat, two-dimensional surface. Your eye begins to search for depth whenever it finds objects juxtaposed.

One of the most intriguing methods of learning to create the illusion of three-dimensional form involves manipulating a neutral form in silhouette. Because the shape is absolute, unaffected by source, direction, or intensity of light, careful attention to the placement of connecting curves and angles is crucial. Figure 3-9 shows silhouetted representations of the three-dimensional forms of a cube, a cylinder, and a pyramid from a variety of viewpoints. Depending on the angle of observation, some representations are ambiguous, some are not. A silhouette becomes ambiguous when it does not suggest one specific figure; the clearest presentation allows a recognizable form to emerge and implies the presence of a ground plane (fig. 3-10).

With the viewpoint established, the silhouette artist manipulates proportional relationships, balancing the space occupied by the figures or objects with the empty space around them. In general, simpler forms create more immediate and dynamic impressions.

Figures 3-11 through 3-14 illustrate the creative process, from source material to final silhouette. After studying the subject, in this case a photograph of a woman standing, you select its dominant characteristics to dramatize. Compare figure 3-12, a traced outline of the model, with figure 3-13, a modified outline, to see why tracing the edge or actual outline of a subject seldom makes a good silhouette. In the first outline, the profile of the model has been flattened somewhat by the distortion of the camera lens. This is especially noticeable at the model's pivot points, such as the twist of her waist and the arm that is bent toward the back. The artist has compensated for this in figure 3-13 by restoring perspective cues to the arm and exaggerating the turn at the model's waist. Notice that the actual exaggeration of form in the finished figure 3-14 has been slight. Additional elements have been added to add interest: the accent of a rectangle in the background to add figure/ground contrast, and the pattern on the shirt to suggest volume.

Figure 3-11. Photograph of a figure standing.

Figure 3-12. Basic outline of the subject, traced from the photograph.

Figure 3-13. Outline of the figure, adjusted to compensate for photographic distortion.

Figure 3-14. Finished silhouette illustration. Details have been added to direct the viewer's interest and define the form three dimensionally. Medium: Pen-and-ink.

EXERCISES

1. Create a crisp, unambiguous silhouette of three related objects with distinct shapes, such as pieces of fruit. Remember to maintain the character of each, arranging the elements so that their shapes do not overlap too much. Do a few thumbnail sketches first, to determine the final arrangement.
2. Find a photograph of a figure in an active pose, and create a silhouette. Pay attention to important details that may be distorted by the camera or lost in the shadows of the photo, and be sure to adjust for them.
3. Repeat exercise 2 using a photograph of two figures interacting.

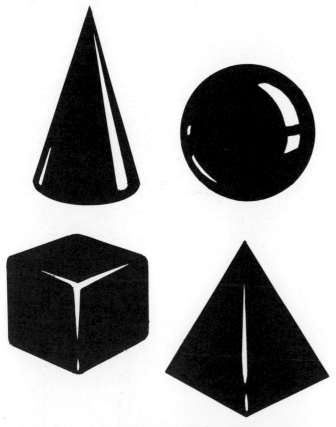

Figure 3-15. For each form, highlights are included to explain the shape most clearly. On the pyramid a linear highlight brings out the forward triangular corner. In the sphere the highlight repeats the nearest external contour. The highlight on the cube follows the vertical and horizontal edges of the planes. Note the direction of the light, which tapers away from the closest corner along the receding edges of the planes.

HIGHLIGHTS

One effective way to convey three dimensionality is to add a minimal highlight to the pure silhouette. With the highlight you introduce a suggestion of space: a clean, concise, and economic gesture defining a form that the silhouette might not communicate otherwise (fig. 3-15). You might also simplify details with stylized highlights to provide variety and graphic interest, as in figure 3-16. Breaking the solid silhouette, introducing negative space and pattern, produces an especially dramatic variation of the basic subject contour (figs. 3-17, 3-18).

EXERCISES

1. Choose an object with reflective surfaces, such as a wine goblet or ceramic vase, and create a highlighted silhouette. Concentrate first on defining the outline as clearly as possible; then add highlights to enhance the form.
2. Create a minimally highlighted silhouette of two chess pieces, stressing the decorative qualities of the highlights. Use an approach similar to that shown in fig. 3-16.

Figure 3-16. *ATM Security Silhouette*, from an article on the technology of security in self-service banking. The highlighted shapes in this silhouette help define the figure and also establish a mysterious atmosphere. Medium: Cut paper. (Illustrator: Renee Gettier-Street)

Figure 3-17. In this student's silhouette illustration, the model's outfit is used to introduce variety to the form. Your eye finishes the torso form by reading the negative space as a blouse. The striped skirt pattern reinforces the figure's movement. (Illustrator: Kathleen Berry)

Figure 3-18. In this student work, the striped skirt on the dancer's costume shows how broad pattern in silhouette can be read as form. (Illustrator: Sharon Pittman)

Figure 3-19. The strong light source in this student's illustration is responsible for almost half of the form. Nevertheless, you can clearly recognize the silhouetted figure and the drama of the subject. Medium: Pen-and-ink. (Illustrator: student, name unknown)

HIGH CONTRAST

Chiaroscuro, translated literally from the Italian, means "light/dark" and is used to describe the technique, popular in late Renaissance and baroque painting, in which contrast between light and shade, without regard to color, produces extreme form contrasts. Applying this device to the silhouette results in a dramatic departure from the traditional black solid (fig. 3-19). The high-contrast silhouette consists of a form in full shadow with extremely sharp-edged highlights. The intricate play of light and dark defines the subject and creates the illusion of three dimensionality (fig. 3-20). A clear differentiation between foreground and background will create a sense of deep space (fig. 3-21).

Designing a high-contrast silhouette is thus a matter of studying the play of bright light from a single source on your subject. Your aim should be to select highlights that will lend meaning to the shadows, both integral (body) and imposed (cast). Rather than depicting every intricate fold and curve, you should simplify the image, exaggerating its features and refining areas of contrast so that shapes are not only descriptive but interesting. Figure 3-23, for example, is a traced outline of its photographic source (fig. 3-22) with the high-contrast areas delineated.

If you compare the working outline in figure 3-23 with the finished illustration of figure 3-24, you will see that, after tracing the edge or actual outline of a subject, you must refine and develop the resulting shape. Slight exaggeration brings the silhouetted form to life. The final high-contrast silhouette successfully suggests the subject's fluidity.

Figure 3-20. Student high-contrast illustration. Working from dark to light is an alternative way of bringing the light source and form together. Medium: Pen-and-ink. (Illustrator: Scott Donohue)

Figure 3-21. *Ski Hidden Valley*, from an information brochure. Two approaches to high-contrast are used in this illustration: the mountains are depicted more or less realistically, while the artist used a stylized linear motif on the couple's faces. Medium: Linocut print. (Illustrator: David Street)

EXERCISES

1. Select a photograph of a figure in a dramatic pose with a strong light source. Create a high-contrast silhouette illustration. First trace the figure in detail, then refine the form, eliminating unnecessary detail. Reduce the shadow contours to light and dark shapes.
2. Repeat the previous exercise using a photograph of two figures interacting.

Figure 3-22. Photograph of a figure in an active pose.

Figure 3-23. Preliminary outline sketch, with the high-contrast areas defined.

Figure 3-24. Finished high-contrast illustration. Medium: Pen-and-ink.

SUGGESTED PORTFOLIO PROJECTS

1. For an article on wildlife sanctuaries, collect pictures of birds suitable for silhouette illustration. Work in a four-inch square format. Simplify and exaggerate detail as necessary to define form.

2. For an article on sport fishing, find pictures of different varieties of fish in profile and create distinctive silhouettes for each.

3. As a space filler in a cooking magazine, create a silhouetted still life from a teapot and teacup or a wine bottle and glass. Pay attention to object size and spatial relationships. Create your own composition from separate sources.

4. Create a silhouette illustrating an episode from a nursery rhyme.

5. For a brochure describing an exhibit on the history of cars, collect pictures of new and vintage automobiles and create highlighted silhouettes. Focus on light from a single direction to simplify the selection of highlighted detail.

6. For a contemporary or a historical romance, create a high-contrast illustration that communicates the passion of a couple in love.

7. Design a mystery-book cover that conveys suspense, using silhouette combined with a few well-placed highlights.

8. Develop a high-contrast illustration for the cover of an annual report, perhaps the exterior of a factory, a grouping of products, or workers gathered around equipment.

CHAPTER 4

LINE TECHNIQUES

Tractor, an illustration for a coloring book. Media: Pen-and-ink, Letratone. (Illustrator: Nigel Holmes)

U sing simple lines, with or without additional texture, an artist can produce versatile, powerful, and expressive drawings. Line art is used widely in print media because it is relatively fast and easy to execute, it reduces or enlarges well, and it is inexpensive to reproduce. Line art will reproduce on the cheapest newsprint, yet it responds with dignity to the fine papers of high-quality magazines. In answer to ever-accelerating production schedules, where illustrations must sometimes be completed in a matter of hours, contemporary artists have largely given up the highly polished look of early-twentieth-century line illustration. Months of detailed sketching and revising have been replaced by new drawing styles that are spontaneous, expressive, and slick (figs. 4-1, 4-2).

A successful line illustrator instills each drawing with a style that both complements and transcends the subject matter. This style is conveyed by the quality of line, which is a matter of technique. Lines have different

Figure 4-1. *Tales from under the Bed*, from a play by the same name. The oval format was chosen because the art was to be surrounded by the accompanying text. Notice the variety of line qualities that make up this illustration. Media: Pen-and-ink on vellum. (Illustrator: Lisa Cypher)

Figure 4-2. *It's Getting a Little Late . . .* , a self-promotional illustration used for stationery, which uses line, stipple, and silhouette. Medium: Pen-and-ink. (Illustrator: Glenn Wolff)

Figure 4-3. Ink lines drawn in various ways, with various pens.

weights (thicknesses), lengths, and characteristics, which are defined by tool, medium, and artist; a change in technique or application of line will often yield a different visual style. To become successful at ink line drawing, you must become familiar with what your tool can do. It is best not to begin drawing until you have practiced creating lines with a variety of tools on a variety of surfaces (fig. 4-3). Try every kind of line—straight, curved, jagged, twisted—in every direction—vertical, horizontal, diagonal. Experiment until you discover methods that reflect your style and produce the desired effects (figs. 4-4, 4-5).

An outline focuses attention on the rendered form. In reality, of course, objects have no lines that bound them. They appear distinct from one another because of differences in brightness or color, and what may appear to be outlines of an object are actually narrow areas of

Figure 4-4. *Kitchen Interior*, from a greeting card, using line and decorative pattern. Medium: Pen-and-ink. (Illustrator: Sarah Sills)

light, shadow, color, and texture. This is true even for relatively sharp changes in form—the angle of a table-top and side, for instance, that results from two planes meeting. For the sake of illustration, though, you must put aside this knowledge in favor of depicting those illusory borderlines.

PEN-AND-INK

Applying pen to paper produces a line that looks, and usually is, final. Your strokes must be bold and confident, your technique grounded in firm knowledge of and practice with the medium. Even if you have confidence in your drawing abilities, working in pen-and-ink can be daunting. It requires broad gestures and movement of the whole forearm, not merely the hand and wrist. The strength and clarity of pen-and-ink lines make the medium perfect for outline illustration as well as a demanding test of coordination (fig. 4-6).

To develop confidence as you practice, lay tracing paper over a master drawing. You can then repeat the same form an unlimited number of times, developing and mastering line qualities without the fear of destroying your drawing (fig. 4-7). Work with a variety of pens, then try brushes for different effects. Also experiment with a variety of papers that vary in surface texture and absorbent qualities.

Tools and Materials. *Pens.* Pens are of five basic types: drawing, quill, lettering, felt-tip, and technical.

Drawing pens are either dip or cartridge style. They have steel nibs of different sizes and shapes that are flexible enough to produce a variety of line widths, depending on the pressure applied. A cartridge pen contains an internal reservoir from which ink is released in a steady flow, which conveniently cuts down on cleaning and refilling. The wooden-handled dip pen is less expensive but requires more care to avoid dripping ink. Each time the pen is dipped, you must allow the excess to run off against the side of the ink bottle and then make test strokes on scrap paper to ensure an even flow. (Remember that the amount of ink on any pen point will affect its, and therefore your, performance.)

Quill pens have small, superfine points good for rendering delicate hairlines in detailed areas. The crow-quill has an especially sharp point, which will dig into the paper surface if pressed too hard.

Lettering pens, although not designed for sketching, are useful for the variety of ink lines they produce. Their nibs, which come in many shapes and sizes, have

Figure 4-5. *Cat's Cradle*, from a greeting card, using a carefully stylized line. Medium: Pen-and-ink. (Illustrator: Jacqueline Gikow)

Figure 4-6. Line illustration of luggage. Media: Crow-quill pen and ink. (Illustrator: Student, name unknown)

broader tips than regular drawing nibs. You can buy angled tips to accommodate either left- or right-handed users.

Designed primarily for tight, precise drawing, *technical pens* each come with a single nib size and produce a line that does not vary in quality. The pen contains an ink reservoir and a fine filament wire in the point that allows a continuous flow of ink. You must hold it at a right angle to the paper, keeping your drawing movement smooth and even to produce a consistent line that does not skip or jump. Technical pens are expensive and require regular cleaning to last; however, frequent use will keep them flowing.

Fine-line felt-tip pens are similar to, but cheaper than, technical pens. Unfortunately, they are not available in many sizes, their ink reservoirs cannot be refilled, and their ink quality is inferior to india ink. Artwork drawn with them fades quickly, making future reproduction a problem.

Ink. Many types of black ink are on the market, but pen-and-ink artists usually use waterproof india ink. An old standby, india ink is a dense black, available in both waterproof and water-soluble formulas (waterproof inks contain a shellac binder so that, once dry, they will not smudge). The quality of india ink varies from brand to brand; you will develop a personal preference based on experience. Inks have also been specially formulated for use in technical pens. These have nonclogging properties and allow the free flow of an ultradense, opaque line.

Paper. Paper surface is the foundation of an illustration because surface texture and absorbency can have a great impact on the overall look of a drawing. Different papers meet different needs, and you will have to do some experimenting to find the kinds of paper most suitable to your drawing personality and to the requirements of an illustration assignment.

As a general rule, for accurate reproduction, pen-and-ink works best with *hot-press paper*. This provides a very smooth, hard surface that keeps the ink line from spreading. Some examples of hot-press papers are plate-finish bristol board and plate-finish illustration board. Prepared acetate or drafting vellums, though not strictly papers, are also acceptable inking surfaces.

Bristol and illustration boards also come in *cold-press* finish, which gives the paper a softer, more textured quality. You may also find other drawing papers suitable for pen-and-ink drawing; be sure they cannot be torn by a pen stroke and do not produce unwanted fuzzy lines.

Figure 4-7. Illustration of foliage, which demonstrates a variety of line qualities resulting from the use of different drawing instruments and hand movement.

EXERCISES

1. Practice gaining control of your hand and pen by drawing sets of straight lines in all directions.
2. Practice drawing lines and creating textures with even and uneven pressure. Use an assortment of pens and brushes to learn how they differ.
3. Choose a simple object, such as a leaf or a teapot, and make a master outline drawing. Using overlays of tracing paper, practice making ink drawings of the same object in ink, changing pens and experimenting with line quality.

VALUE

If you squint while looking at a black-and-white photograph, you can distinguish shades of gray. These gray shades, called *values*, give three-dimensional images portrayed in black-and-white their depth and definition. One way of learning to define values in an object is to make a simple outline drawing of an object and then break down the form into distinct areas of light and shade. You began this process in high-contrast silhouette when you divided form into two values, white and black, by simplifying essential patterns of light.

Mapping is an analytical technique that can be used to identify contrasting light and shadow. In this approach you group and outline a few clearly defined values, keeping the patterns as large and simple as the subject allows. The resulting drawing will have a topographical look (figs. 4-8, 4-9).

With an outline drawing, you can describe the shape and perhaps the basic details of your subject, but to introduce values to create a sense of depth, you must incorporate linear texture. Almost any pattern (dots, dashes, circles, curlicues, squiggles, scribbles), repeated over and over with increasing and decreasing density, will simulate light and shade, creating values. The examples in figure 4-10 show only a few of the patterns and values possible by varying the pressure, spacing, and curves of pen lines.

CROSSHATCHING

Crosshatched lines are parallel lines that intersect with other parallel lines to simulate light, shade, and/or texture. You can form crosshatch lines either mechanically, using a ruler or straightedge, or freely, by hand,

Figure 4-8. Photograph of a face. (Photo: Robert Herman)

Figure 4-9. The strong lighting of the woman's face in figure 4-8 allows a clear mapping of lit and shadowed areas.

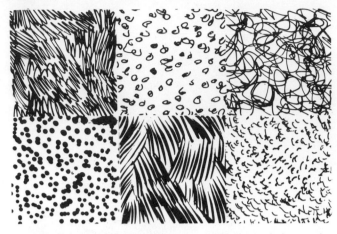

Figure 4-10. Examples of dots, squiggles, and other line work that may be used to depict texture and tonal value.

as shown in figure 4-11. The length, width, shape, and direction of lines may vary. The key to becoming adept at crosshatching is learning to apply the values skillfully, using a patient, methodical approach. Begin with the lightest areas and gradually work up to the darkest ones to achieve an even gradation (fig. 4-12).

EXERCISES

1. On a piece of plate bristol board, draw an eight-inch square. Divide that into nine two-inch squares, leaving a one-inch margin around each box. Use the boxes to experiment with pen-and-ink textures and values. Try a variety of pens, making your lines straight, curved, zigzag, and crosshatched.

2. On a piece of plate bristol board, draw two rectangles six inches long and two inches wide. Working from top to bottom, practice ruled crosshatching in the first rectangle. Divide the strip into six one-inch sections. Leave the top section white, and paint the bottom section black. Using a straightedge and a technical pen, cover the four remaining one-inch sections with even horizontal lines. Of these four, cover the bottom three with even vertical lines. Then cover the bottom two sections with right-diagonal lines. Finally, draw left-diagonal lines in the empty top section. This will result in a gray-scale strip.

   In the second rectangle, again working from top to bottom, create a value strip of freehand cross-hatched lines, using the same hatching as in the first rectangle, drawn without a straightedge. Aim for at least five distinct values, from light to solid black.

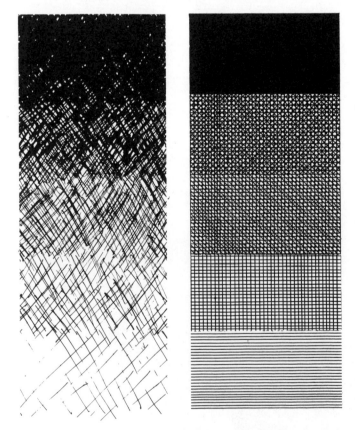

Figure 4-11. Examples of freehand and mechanical crosshatching, executed on a value scale from white to black.

Figure 4-12. *Alice Walker.* This portrait series of the writer appeared in the *Christian Science Monitor* surrounding a profile of her work. Proceeding down from upper left and then from upper right, the techniques employed are: pure line with mapping of shadow; mechanical crosshatching; mechanical lines in high-contrast silhouette; texture and contoured crosshatching; scribbled texture; and freehand crosshatching. Medium: Pen-and-ink. (Illustrator: Chuck McVicker)

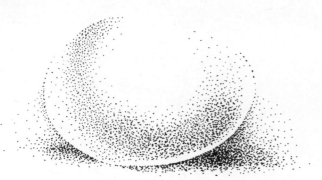

Figure 4-13. Stippled illustration of an egg. Light and shadow are indicated by the density of stippling. Medium: Pen-and-ink. (Illustrator: Scott Pinkava)

Figure 4-14. Stippled illustration of a broken egg shell, showing that the shell has a distinct thickness. Medium: Pen-and-ink. (Illustrator: Scott Pinkava)

Stippling. Stippling involves bouncing your pen gently on the paper with a stiff-arm motion to create small dots of ink. You spread ink dots thinly to create light values and concentrate them densely to create dark values. Although this technique is time consuming, the results are appealing; a stippled image resembles a screened halftone image used for reproducing photographs in print (fig. 4-13).

To learn the technique, practice creating the image of a smooth, contoured surface. Use a pen with a stiff point such as a crow-quill, a felt-tip, or a technical pen; the last is ideal for making dots and dot contouring because it renders all the dots in the same size and shape. Begin by placing each stipple dot in a precise spatial order. Lightly stipple the entire drawing and then build up the darker tones by adding more dots. As you close gaps, be careful not to overstipple, or your work will become too dark.

Although stipples may seem to be placed at random, a successful illustration is the product of careful planning (fig. 4-14). Place stipples in lines only when that arrangement is meaningful, perhaps to define form or thickness (fig. 4-15). You might also use stippling to define or enhance only one or two details of a drawing. Try uneven spacing or different-sized dots to create the appearance of rough surfaces (fig. 4-16).

Figure 4-15. *Marilyn*, a student illustration using stippling. Medium: Pen-and-ink. (Illustrator: Douglas Reinke)

Figure 4-16. *Don't Drink the Water*. Stipple illustration for an article on the pollution of drinking water. Medium: Pen-and-ink. (Illustrator: Glenn Wolff; art director: Patrick J. B. Flynn)

EXERCISES

1. Draw a two-inch square and fill it with dots that are more or less equally spaced. Apply even pressure to the pen so that the dots are of uniform weight as well. Strive for an even overall value.
2. Using the stipple technique, create a value scale in a one- by four-inch strip. Aim to create five distinct values.
3. Draw an egg to practice stippling a three-dimensional form. First indicate the egg's contour in light pencil. Then begin stippling the lightest tones, building up the dots to create darker values and contours.

PENCIL

"Lead" pencils are actually filled with a combination of graphite and clay. The degree of hardness or softness of a graphite pencil depends on the amount of clay used in its manufacture. The less clay in the mixture, the softer the lead; the softer the lead, the darker its color. Most pencils come in seventeen degrees of hardness. The letter *H* designates hard leads, ranging from H to 8H, which is the hardest. *B* designates soft leads, with 8B the softest. In between is an HB lead. For most illustrations, you need only 2H, HB, and 2B pencils.

The key to successful pencil rendering is maintaining line freshness, which means starting with a sharp pencil and sharpening as necessary. Softer grades of lead will require frequent sharpening, but this hardly detracts from the ease and economy of working with pencil.

From simple doodles to sophisticated drawings, you can execute the same line techniques in pencil that you can with pen-and-ink. With pencil, however, you can achieve a wide range of effects by changing the paper texture. You can vary the lines by changing drawing speed and hand pressure (fig. 4-17), and you can erase and correct your work. Erasing completely is one way of introducing highlights (figs. 4-18, 4-19).

Pencil types include drawing, Ebony, carpenter's, and graphite drawing sticks.

Drawing (or writing) *pencils* have graphite cores encased in round or hexagonal wooden barrels. A variation is the *mechanical pencil*, which is refillable and comes with different barrel sizes and lead diameters. A spring mechanism regulates the lead feed, so you never have to sharpen.

Figure 4-17. A wide range of tonal and pattern effects can be achieved with one pencil. The pencil can be used to create an endless variety of ruled, dotted, hatched, or scribbled textures.

Figure 4-18. *A Foreign Affair*, from an article on the cross-cultural benefits of hosting foreign exchange students. Medium: Pencil. (Illustrator: Kathleen Volp)

Ebony pencils, with graphite cores a little wider than those of drawing pencils, are excellent for freehand sketching as well as finished rendering. These pencils have a fine-quality soft, jet-black graphite that produces a very smooth line. They easily produce both light and dark tones.

Carpenter's pencils are long, flat sketching tools with a graphite core about one-eighth inch thick. You must sharpen the flat lead (available in 2B, 4B, and 6B) by hand using a razor blade, which produces a variety of points.

Graphite drawing sticks are pieces of graphite without barrels, three inches long and one-quarter inch square. By applying the long edge of the graphite stick to paper, you can produce a very wide stroke.

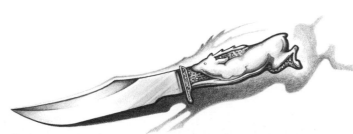

Figure 4-19. *Sharpening up on the Art of Knife-Making*, from a newspaper article on knife making. In developing this image, the artist sought to meld various aspects—beauty, function, the user—of the knife. She recalled hunting fetishes and rituals of certain cultures. The knife here becomes an empowered object in its own right. Medium: Pencil. (Illustrator: Kathleen Volp)

Paper. Almost every surface and texture accepts pencil and suits some form of line illustration. Begin with tracing paper and two-ply vellum-finish bristol board, then experiment with a range of papers.

Erasers. Among the many types of erasers on the market, the two best suited for pencil work are the kneaded rubber eraser and the white plastic eraser. You can form the pliable kneaded eraser into shapes perfect for picking up specific areas of graphite, while the white plastic eraser is a general-purpose eraser, good for removing large areas of graphite from the paper surface. It can also be cut into precise shapes and used as a tool to introduce highlights into a drawing by erasing pencil tones in defined areas.

Fixative. A spray medium that protects dry media such as pencil from being smudged or rubbed off when touched, fixative is either workable or permanent. Workable fixative has a matte finish that protects your drawing as you work. Permanent fixative has a glossy waterproof finish that seals the drawing and prevents further application of graphite. A medium coating of workable fixative works fine as the final fix of a drawing, however, so you need not purchase the permanent type.

EXERCISES

1. Gain control of your hand and pencil by drawing sets of straight lines in all directions.
2. Practice drawing lines and creating textures with even and uneven pressure. Use pencils of different degrees of hardness.
3. Choose a few simple subjects, and make a few spot pencil illustrations. Simplify light and shade into broad areas of form and texture.

SHADING FILMS

Many graphic-art suppliers sell shading or tone films, commonly known by the trademark name Zip-A-Tone, sometimes also called benday sheets. These films are sheets of a low-tack, adhesive-backed plastic, printed with many different patterns, including crosshatching, strips, dots, random textures, and architectural textures (bricks, water, wood). They are available with either black or white patterns, in varying densities, for use on light- or dark-colored backgrounds. Illustrators find preprinted shading films useful for completing illustrations quickly and for varying the illustration style within a drawing (fig. 4-20).

Before applying shading film to a drawing, plan its placement carefully: it must fit into well-defined areas with hard edges. If you choose to use more than one value, note the locations on a rough drawing to avoid making mistakes. And if the artwork is going to be reduced in reproduction, choose a coarse pattern to prevent the texture from becoming too fine.

Using a sharp no. 11 blade in an X-Acto knife, with a light but sure hand, cut a piece of shading film slightly larger than the size of the area you want to cover (fig. 4-21). Do not cut through the backing sheet. Peel off the protective backing, and lay the film in position. Be careful not to apply a lot of pressure when you lay the film down on the illustration, or it will be difficult to remove the extra material. Cut away the excess film, then lay a piece of tracing paper over the illustration and burnish the film to remove air bubbles.

SCRATCHBOARD

Scratchboard consists of white cardboard coated with heavy white clay, which is then coated with india ink. To "draw" with this medium, you scratch off the ink to reveal the clay, producing white lines in the black surface (figs. 4-22, 4-23). All of the line techniques previously discussed can be used on scratchboard. Because

Figure 4-20. *The Morning Ride,* from an article on bicycle commuting. Media: Pen-and-ink, shading film. (Illustrator: Jacqueline Gikow)

Figure 4-21. To apply shading film: (*A*) Cut a small section of the shading film. (*B*) Position the shading film. (*C*) Cut away the excess film. (*D*) Cut out the desired area; then rub the film with a spoon-tip burnisher. (Illustrator: Scott Pinkava)

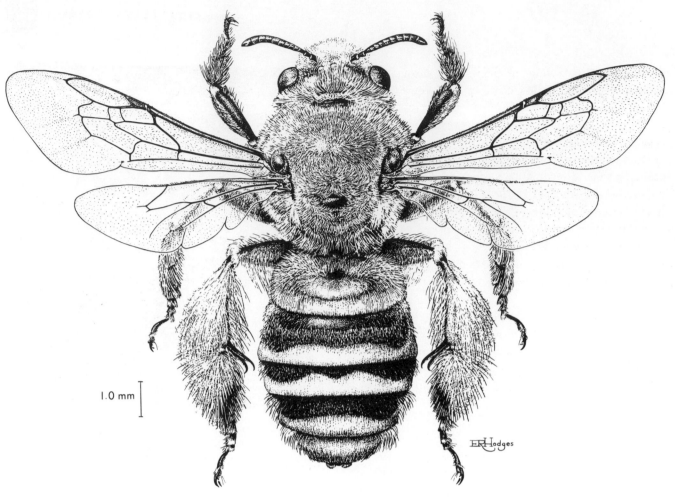

Figure 4-22. This illustration of a bee, *Diadasia rinconis*, was used in a research paper. The composition represents a standard habitus view of an insect. Reference for the illustration was a dry pinned bee viewed through a microscope. A detailed preliminary drawing was checked by the scientist-author. The final drawing was transferred to white scratchboard and rendered by painting black the parts into which white lines were to be scratched. Media: Ink and scratchboard. (Illustrator: Elaine R. S. Hodges; author: Ronald J. McGinley, Smithsonian Institution)

Figure 4-23. *Wonderful Town*, for a book review of an anthology of famous impressions of New York. Dramatic lighting and perspective are used to develop a theatrical theme and enhance the chorus-line motif. Medium: Scratchboard. (Illustrator: Ruth Lozner)

the line work is white on black, you must think in reverse. Instead of adding shadows, you create the highlights of the drawing. For example, dense crosshatching produces light values, while spare crosshatching leaves an area dark (fig. 4-24).

Scratchboard comes in two weights, professional and a lighter, lower-quality student grade. Your design will determine whether you will choose a prepared (pre-inked) or unprepared surface. If your subject has a black background or a lot of dark areas, prepared scratchboard will be your best choice. For a drawing with a white background or many light areas, an unprepared surface saves you the tedious job of removing large areas of ink.

To prepare your own scratchboard, first mount the unprepared board on a piece of stiff backing, using rubber cement. Lightly sketch your design in pencil, and then fill in the outline with india ink, using short, quick brush strokes. Let the first coat dry, and then apply a second.

You can use almost any sharp instrument—a pin, an X-Acto knife, an etching needle, a single-edge razor blade—as a scratching tool. Art supply stores sell inexpensive tools that hold small pointed knives. The tips come in a variety of styles, including multipointed ones for drawing several parallel lines at once. Feel free to experiment: a distinct advantage of scratchboard is that mistakes can be easily corrected by brushing on more ink.

The best way to work is toward yourself, rotating the board as necessary to maintain a comfortable hand position. Use light pressure to remove the ink, because scratching all the way down to the paper surface will weaken the higher clay ridges and leave the clay surface vulnerable to cracking.

Figure 4-24. Demonstration of scratchboard technique on prepared scratchboard: *left:* a value strip of textures; *right:* a simple illustration.

EXERCISES

1. On a piece of prepared scratchboard, practice crosshatching and inventing textures with various cutting tools.
2. On a second piece, make a test strip of crosshatching that includes five distinct values.
3. On a piece of unprepared scratchboard, draw a simple three-dimensional subject, such as an apple. Paint the object's silhouette in ink, and then cut the form, introducing linear texture and value.

Figure 4-25. *Alcohol Rehab*, one of a series of collage illustrations used to illustrate a book of poems. This illustration also accompanied a newspaper article on alcohol rehabilitation centers. Medium: Paper collage using engravings. (Illustrator: Joan Hall)

OTHER MEDIA

Although this chapter has discussed line drawing with traditional media, many alternatives are available for developing a line illustration style that is distinctive and personal. Some of them have been reproduced earlier in this chapter. Included are wood and linoleum cuts, intaglio print methods, monoprints, photocopies, and cut paper or collage. Figure 4-25 shows a distinctive, personal application of a nontraditional line illustration.

SUGGESTED PORTFOLIO PROJECTS

1. To fill space in a magazine, create an expressive line illustration of a basic object, such as an interesting chair, hat, or bottle.

2. To fill space in a cooking magazine, draw three vegetables or kitchen utensils. Arrange the objects in a variety of ways, making thumbnails and roughs that reflect different points of view, close-up and from a distance. Prepare three pen-and-ink renderings: pure line, line and texture (using free texture or crosshatching), and stippling.

3. Using a tool that will produce a strong line, such as a .50 technical pen or a felt-tip pen, create three line illustrations that depict a simple procedure, such as threading a sewing needle, planting a seedling, or tying a shoe.

4. Choose a photograph of a fashion figure in a magazine, and create a line illustration that enhances the model's outfit. Create impact by accentuating parts of the outfit and leaving other parts less defined. Combine line with stippling.

5. Using drawn lines and shading films, create an illustration that brings out the most important characteristics of a complicated product, such as a car or a computer.

6. Execute a clearly recognizable stipple portrait of a famous person.

7. Working in pencil, draw a cleaning implement or a shop tool for a newspaper advertisement. As you render the product, strive for a realistic contrast of light and shade, and eliminate unnecessary detail.

8. Use pencil to create an illustration depicting a person using a product: a woman eating a hot dog, a child holding a stuffed animal, a teenager flying a kite, a man reading a book.

9. On either prepared or unprepared scratchboard, create an illustration for the book-review section of a periodical: draw a row of books so that some are upright and some are in piles.

10. Select an article or short story from a magazine, and provide a line illustration that conveys enough information about the piece to pique a reader's interest. Use a variety of line techniques.

John O'Hara—Famous Pennsylvania Author. One of sixteen illustrations commissioned for an educational series on famous Pennsylvania writers published in state newspapers. Media: Graphite and Dr. Martin's gray dyes on Strathmore. (Illustrator: Frederick H. Carlson)

N ot surprisingly, watercolor is usually considered a color medium. But its sense of implied light and depth, its subtlety and range, can be just as evident, just as compelling, when used only in black-and-white. The qualities of water—wet, flowing, liquid, tactile—combine with the illustrator's objectives—communication of mood, energy, and capturing the moment. Transparent watercolor and inks are challenging media because the process of painting is visible and somewhat unpredictable, and alterations are difficult to make. Opaque water-based paints, such as acrylic or gouache, applied either with brush or airbrush, offer more control. Both can add rich dimension and vitality to monochromatic illustrations.

WASHES

A wash is a thin application of ink or paint, transparent or opaque, most often with a brush. The look of a partic-

Figure 5-1. Portrait of the folksinger Norman Blake, published in *Foxfire*. The artist used the images of the guitar player to evoke the sense of the music building to a climax. The blocks of wash act as a foundation for the more specific drawing. Media: Graphite and watercolor dyes. (Illustrator: Frederick H. Carlson)

ular wash depends on the combination of brush, pigment (the basis of tonal value), water (the vehicle that carries pigment in greater or lesser concentration), and ground (surface). In general, transparent washes have a looser, more painterly feeling and look, while opaque surfaces are more effective when they are applied to tightly rendered illustrations. Illustrations can be created with washes alone or in combination with ink lines (figs. 5-1, 5-2).

Using line and wash together allows you to combine two effects: the lines provide definition and structure, while the washes direct the viewer's attention to a specific area, introduce shadow, texture, or value, and add decorative interest (fig. 5-3). Illustrators normally use waterproof india ink to create the line art so that the lines and wash remain distinct, but you can obtain interesting effects by doing the line drawing in water-soluble ink and letting it run into the wash. You can also experiment with applying wash applications before adding ink lines.

Ground. Although you can execute wash illustrations on watercolor paper, illustration board, and prepared acetate, choosing the most appropriate surface is important because the color and texture of the paper may

Figure 5-2. *Lunch at the Museum of Natural History*, from an article on new restaurants in New York museums. This illustration shows the richness that can be achieved by breaking down objects and space into planes of light and shadow to build forms. Medium: Watercolor. (Illustrator: Doris Ettlinger)

Figure 5-3. *Broken Bones,* a line and wash illustration published in *Today's Parent* for an article on children's injuries. Media: Pen-and-ink and watercolor wash. (Illustrator: Anne Weisz)

remain visible in reproduction. In fact, in transparent wash, the color of the paper is supposed to show through, and you may leave the paper untouched by wash where the brightest highlights should be. Watercolor paper comes in hot-press (smooth), cold-press (medium), and rough textures. Illustrators most frequently use a cold-press paper surface for transparent wash illustration because it has enough texture to prevent running and allows you to work rapidly. Washes on hot-press papers tend to have hard edges, which may or may not suit a particular work.

Acetate is sometimes used as an overlay to introduce wash into a line drawing that has been completed on paper. Washes executed on acetate have similar qualities to washes done on hot-press paper. The advantage to doing a wash on an acetate overlay is that the illustration can be reproduced as line art (without the overlay) and as a halftone (with the overlay).

Brushes. Brushes, like pens, come in many varieties, numbered to define size: the lower the number, the finer the brush. The two major types of brushes are round and flat. Round brushes are full-bodied brushes that come to a fine point. Since they hold a lot of liquid, they

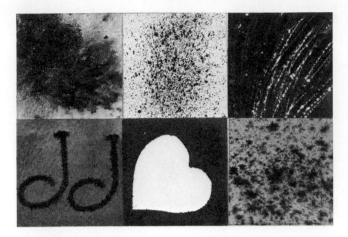

Figure 5-4. Examples of special effects produced using diluted india ink. From left to right, *top:* crystallized salt application, toothbrush spatter, scratched paper surface; *bottom:* stamping, masking, toothbrush spatter on wet surface.

do not require frequent dipping in water or pigment. Flat (sometimes called sky) brushes are best for large areas of wash and for backgrounds. You can use lettering brushes as well, but they tend to be very expensive because they contain more hair than most brushes.

Its softness and flexibility make red sable the best brush material—and also the most expensive. A number of good-quality imitation-sable brushes are available that are less expensive than red sable. In the case of flat brushes, a good synthetic is actually preferable because it offers more bounce and control. Avoid inferior camels'-hair and student-quality brushes when doing professional work.

Choose a brush whose size is appropriate for the area to be completed. Using a brush that is too small will result in streaking because thin strokes of pigment will dry before you are finished. For most wash painting, you need only three brushes: one medium-sized round brush (size 3 to 7), a large round brush (size 9 to 14), and a flat brush (three-quarters to one inch). As you gain expertise, however, you may want to add brushes that provide more control, and experiment with cardboard shapes, rubber stamps, sponges, and found objects to produce diverse effects. You can create other effects with masks, available in liquid or paper, that cover areas to be left white (fig. 5-4).

Brushes wear well and last for a long time when they are properly treated. Always keep the brush handle down in an empty container. Do not leave them sitting in water while you are working because the glue that holds the hairs in the brush holder will loosen. Rinse brushes with a mild detergent after you finish, and let them dry naturally.

Pigment. To mix pigment with water, you will need three to five small containers or a palette, which can be plastic, metal, or porcelain. Also fill a large container with water for rinsing out your brushes.

Ink. Diluting ink with water allows you to create gray tones. With practice you will learn to judge the right combination of pigment and water to achieve a desired value (fig. 5-5). A permanent medium, india ink cannot be reworked after it dries.

Watercolor. Watercolor paints dry more slowly than ink and afford you more time to render. Additionally, they can be dampened and lifted off to some degree, even after drying.

Transparent watercolors come in solid cakes, tubes, and bottles. The solid cakes of color come in palette sets in a self-closing box. These solid pan colors need a drop

Figure 5-5. Cubes rendered in: (*top*) graded transparent wash; (*middle*) flat transparent wash, creating three tones; (*bottom*) opaque flat wash.

of water added to each cake several minutes before use to soften the pigment. Tubes, which are sold either individually or in sets, contain pigment that is already soft and moist. Liquid watercolor and dyes come in bottles with eyedropper tops, which release a small amount of highly concentrated pigment.

Figure 5-6. *Headin' off Down the Road,* illustration for the book *Jump On Over!* about the adventures of Brer Rabbit and his family. Medium: Transparent watercolor. (Illustrator: Barry Moser; © Pennyroyal Press, Inc.)

Opaque water-based paint, or *gouache*, is a good-quality dense paint that produces a smooth, even surface. In addition to "designer colors," you can buy tubes of white and black, as well as premixed gray tones that facilitate rendering camera-ready art.

Gouache from the tube is usually too concentrated to apply directly to an illustration. Prepare gouache for painting by diluting it with water, mixing until it is of brushing consistency (about the thickness of heavy cream). Begin by creating the lightest tones first. As you add black to the white mixture, blend the pigments together until no streaks are visible. To ensure streakless washes, thoroughly premix the paint in the palette before painting it on the paper.

Techniques. Adding wash to a drawing is akin to filling in a coloring book, in that each tone occupies a distinct area adjacent to lighter and darker tones (fig. 5-6). The key to a successful wash is to keep it fresh. Overworking a wash will cause muddiness and decrease the tonal contrast. Proper planning is essential, since you will not have time to deliberate once you begin. Clearly delineate the shape of the wash, and if the outline is intricate, consider using liquid frisket to mask out the shape so it can be brushed with speed. Along with careful planning, success with washes depends on mastery of two techniques, the flat wash and the graded wash.

Flat Wash. The classic watercolor technique, this method requires a tilted board so that gravity aids the flow of pigment. Creating small, even wash areas is not difficult, but covering a large area smoothly requires more skill. The secret is to do the wash all at once, fairly quickly, so that none of the strokes dry before the wash is finished.

A wash should be floated on, rather than rubbed in. Each wash stroke should overlap the previous one, leaving a slight bead of pigment running along the bottom of each stroke (fig. 5-7). Beginning at one place, stopping, and starting somewhere else will cause an uneven

Figure 5-7. Applying a flat watercolor wash. (*A*) First brush stroke; the darker area along the bottom of the stroke indicates where the bead of wet pigment was left. (*B*) Second brush stroke; each stroke overlays the previous stroke. (*C*) Additional brush strokes, each using the bead of pigment for an even application. (*D*) Finished flat wash.

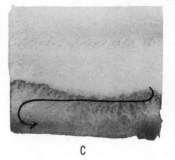

Figure 5-8. *Moose*, an illustration for a full-page ad to promote a wildlife film series. Reference photographs were supplied by the client; the artist also sketched directly from a museum exhibit of moose and took additional snapshots for further reference. Medium: Gouache. (Illustrator: Rick Barry)

Figure 5-9. A flat opaque wash, showing five different gray values.

shade. Working from top to bottom, again taking advantage of the effects of gravity, helps to ensure even coverage. If the wash is too light, you can build it up after the first wash has dried completely by laying on another flat-wash layer in the same manner. It is preferable to start with a lighter wash because it is difficult to lighten a too-dark wash.

You apply opaque wash in a similar way (fig. 5-8). Begin at the top and apply the paint smoothly, with slightly overlapping strokes. However, to achieve a flat, even tone, first apply a thin layer horizontally, and after that layer dries, add a vertical layer. Repeat this procedure until you create a solid tone (fig. 5-9).

Graded Wash. This technique requires somewhat more control than a smooth wash does. Again working on a tilted board, load your brush with a dark pigment-and-water mixture and make one or two overlapping horizontal strokes. For the next stroke, load the brush with water only. Continue dipping the brush into clear water to dilute the pigment, creating a gradual transition from dark to light with each consecutive overlapping stroke (fig. 5-5). You may find it difficult to achieve such smoothly graded shading with a brush and opaque paints, because these pigments dry very quickly, so try a hard-edged gradation of tones instead.

EXERCISES

1. Mark off seven squares, each approximately three inches in size. Leave the first square white and paint the last square black. In the remaining boxes, create a value chart with a series of five flat transparent washes, each a separate gray tone. Aim to create values that are evenly graded in steps from pale gray to deep charcoal. Do this exercise using watercolor and then again with india ink.
2. Try to create different values by layering a single wash. Begin by painting a three-inch flat wash. When the square dries, paint over half to create a second layer. When that layer dries, build up a third tone.
3. Practice creating graded washes: (a) begin with the darkest value and work to the lightest; (b) begin with the lightest value and work to the darkest; (c) begin with a light value, work to a dark, and then back to a light value again; and (d) begin with a dark value, work to a light, and back to a dark value again.
4. Mark off seven squares, each approximately two inches in size. Leave the first square white, and paint the last square black. In the remaining squares create a value chart with a series of five flat opaque washes, each a separate tone. Aim to create values that are evenly graded from pale gray to deep charcoal. You will probably have to paint more than five gray samples to achieve an even change in value from light to dark.

AIRBRUSH

Beginning illustrators often approach the airbrush with awe, even trepidation. And while airbrush techniques can be both complicated and time consuming, they enable you to create effects difficult to match with other tools (fig. 5-10). Learning to use an airbrush is a matter of practice and experimentation. Expect to go through a lot of paper doing basic exercises before you feel confident about the results.

A sophisticated piece of equipment, the airbrush mixes pigment with air to produce a soft texture without

Figure 5-10. Illustration used in an ad for a golf resort community. Medium: Airbrush with transparent inks. (Illustrator: David McKelvey)

brush strokes or drawing marks. It allows you to blend tones gradually so that it is hard to tell where one ends and another begins. You can use it as a spray gun to cover a broad area in wash, or you can focus its flow to yield a line as fine as that of a soft pencil. You can also create crisp images through the use of stencils and masks.

Mastering the tool itself is only half the battle, however. Airbrushing, more than any other illustration technique, calls for meticulous planning of pigment application. Once the process is underway, you have little room for last-minute changes. Even advanced airbrush

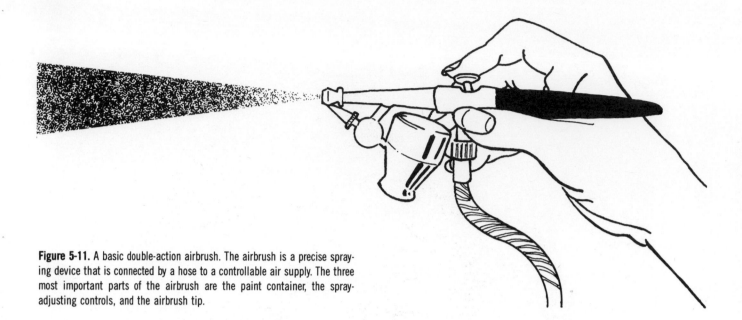

Figure 5-11. A basic double-action airbrush. The airbrush is a precise spraying device that is connected by a hose to a controllable air supply. The three most important parts of the airbrush are the paint container, the spray-adjusting controls, and the airbrush tip.

illustrators attempt to perfect planned effects before approaching final works.

Pigment flow is adjustable in two ways: by increasing or decreasing the amount of air, and by opening or closing the nozzle that controls paint flow (fig. 5-11). A *single-action* airbrush, the least expensive professional model, has a lever that controls only the supply of air; you must adjust the nozzle manually. In a *double-action* airbrush, the finger lever controls both air (up and down) and paint flow (forward or back).

Of the numerous airbrushes on the market, the Paasche H Series, model H-1, is a good learning tool. It accepts both small color cups and three-fluid-ounce jars, and it can be used for fine lines as well as broader sprays. Perhaps most important, the Paasche H has few parts, so it is easy to clean. Because you have to clean your airbrush before use, during the working process, and after you have finished, this medium often seems to involve more preparation and maintenance than other kinds of illustration.

Propellant Systems. In addition to the airbrush, you need an air supply and a flexible hose to attach the two. The brand of airbrush and type of propellant you use will dictate to some extent the choice of hose. Be sure that the hose attaches to both or that you purchase the necessary adapters.

Begin with one of the two most basic, practical, and inexpensive types of propellant. A can of compressed air, available at most art supply stores, will provide about twenty minutes of spraying time. Its pressure is adequate and fairly even for most of the contents, and it works quietly. Always keep a spare can of propellant in reserve to ensure sufficient air to finish a job.

For about the cost of twenty disposable cans of air, you can buy a small, portable compressor. This is a more satisfactory instrument for general use. You will find a moisture filter useful for minimizing the pulsing vibration characteristic of these machines.

Pigment. In general, you can run almost any liquid medium with an airbrush. Water-based media, such as india ink, transparent watercolor, and gouache, are the easiest to prepare and to clean up. You can use a brush for loading pigment into the color cup, but an eyedropper will prove far more efficient.

Paper. A variety of surfaces, including special airbrush boards, work well with the airbrush. Two-ply vellum-surfaced bristol board or cold-press illustration board are excellent surfaces, which allow you to combine airbrush with other techniques, such as pen-and-ink or pencil.

Masking. A mask prevents the airbrush spray from hitting your drawing surface. It can be as simple as a piece of torn newspaper or a more durable cardboard stencil, but the primary type of mask is film frisket, which comes in sheets or rolls. A thin, transparent plastic with a low-tack adhesive backing that will not tear your paper when removed, frisket consistently gives a hard edge to your spraying. (Liquid frisket, that can be painted on and peeled off, is also available.)

To use a frisket, cut a piece slightly larger than the dimensions of your drawing. Peel off the waxed paper, and lay the frisket paper down on the drawing. Using an X-Acto knife with a sharp no. 11 blade, cut along the outlines of your drawing, making sure to cut only the frisket and not the paper surface. This skill requires some practice, so that you neither cut too deeply and score the drawing ground nor cut too lightly and cause the frisket to tear when removed.

If you plan your airbrush illustration well, you avoid the tedious job of removing frisket from certain areas of your work and then trying to return it to its original position. Instead, plan your work so that each time you remove a section of frisket, you overspray the last plane, applying progressive layers of pigment. Begin by spraying what will be the darkest and proceed to the lightest planes (figs. 5-12, 5-13, 5-14). Begin and end the brush movement well outside the boundaries of a frisket stencil to avoid blotching.

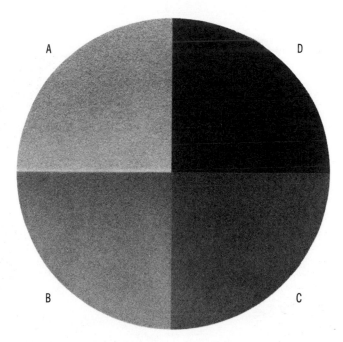

Figure 5-12. Examples of four different airbrushed values that demonstrate the overspray technique. (*A*) The first plane is sprayed with a light wash. (*B*) The first and second planes are sprayed, resulting in a darker first plane and a light second plane. (*C*) The third plane is sprayed, and the first and second are oversprayed. (*D*) the entire sphere is sprayed, resulting in four distinct, flat, airbrushed tones.

Figure 5-13. *Neige*, a self-promotional airbrush illustration. The facial features and broad, graded background plane are airbrushed, while the flat planes of color have been cut from adhesive-backed plastic film. Media: Airbrush with Spectralite acrylics, gray Pantone films. (Illustrator: Elvira Regine)

Figure 5-14. *Auto Land*, an unpublished illustration using the overspray technique. Medium: Airbrush with india ink. (Illustrator: Jacqueline Gikow)

Spray Techniques. An airbrush releases small particles of paint into the air, which could be harmful to breathe (even water-based paints are hazardous). As a precaution, make sure to work in a ventilated room, wear a disposable painter's mask, and take frequent breaks from your work to breathe fresh air.

Along with the finger control button, the distance that you hold the airbrush from the paper will affect the quality of spray, which will be concentrated at close range and diffused when farther away. Adjust the spray on scrap paper before you begin. Experiment with the control button, air pressure, and distance from the paper until you make a satisfactory mark (fig. 5-15). For best results keep the airbrush one to six inches from the paper, and spray using an even motion, passing your hand across the artwork at a constant distance from the paper. Learn to judge that space, and develop the habit of keeping your wrist stiff. Beginners have a tendency to dip—that is, to begin at one level, drop down in the middle of the sweep, and raise the hand up again at the end.

Lines. With a pencil, rule off a series of horizontal lines about one inch apart; then practice making fine, even lines. Begin with a few "dummy" passes (no paint or pressure) at your line, keeping your airbrush an even distance one to four inches from the ground. Once you have the feel of it, load your airbrush with ink, turn on the air pressure, and spray a real line.

Start the spray once your hand is in motion. Follow the path you determined in practice, but stop the spray before you stop your hand movement. Starting or stopping the spray when your hand is at rest will cause a thick blotch of ink to form at either end of the line. Since each airbrush requires a different touch, you should practice making lines at different distances until you can achieve consistent results.

Washes. As with watercolors, executing an airbrush wash requires smooth movement; position the spraying surface at a slight angle to facilitate even spraying. Hold the airbrush four to six inches from the paper to achieve various large, even tones; again, avoid starting and stopping the spray during a single pass. Do not try to achieve the full intensity of tone in one pass of the airbrush; instead, use a few layers of wash to build it up. Of course, a broad "spread tone" requires greater air pressure and volume of ink than that needed to produce a fine line (fig. 5-16).

To create an evenly graded wash, lessen the pressure on the finger lever and move the airbrush away from the drawing surface as you progress down the wash area. Apply more layers of pigment at the top, or darker end, of the wash than at the bottom.

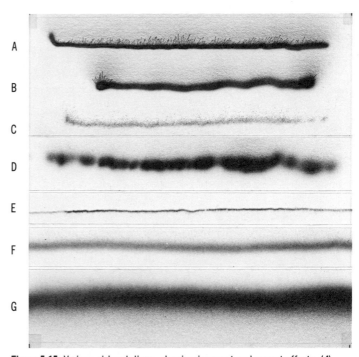

Figure 5-15. Various airbrush lines, showing incorrect and correct effects. (*A*) Centipede effect: the airbrush has been held too close to the paper for the amount of ink and pressure being applied. (*B*) Blobs: the paint was released before the hand began moving and/or the hand was stopped before the pressure was stopped. (*C*) Grainy spray: Either the pigment has not been diluted sufficiently with water or there was insufficient air pressure. (*D*) Blotchy line: Uneven pressure was applied to the pressure control button. (*E*, *F*, *G*) Lines drawn correctly as the airbrush was gradually moved away from the paper.

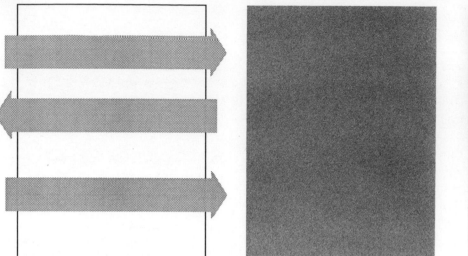

Figure 5-16. The correct movement of the airbrush across a plane, followed by examples of a smooth airbrush wash and a graded airbrush wash.

Figure 5-17. Signature created with a controlled airbrush spray.

EXERCISES

1. Once you can draw a line to any thickness, practice signing your name (fig. 5-17). Give yourself a lot of room, and begin with a large signature.
2. Cut a three- by four-inch rectangular-shaped frisket mask and place it over a fresh piece of paper. Holding your airbrush about six to eight inches from the paper, spray continuously and horizontally, left to right and then right to left, moving gradually down the rectangle. (Remember to spray over the edges to avoid blotching at the boundaries.) The arrowed diagram in figure 5-16 illustrates the movement of the airbrush over the image.
3. Draw a small (approximately three inches) line figure in ink. Cut a frisket to cover the illustration, and create a rectangular frame of flat airbrush wash around it. Aim for a 50 percent gray value, about halfway between white and black.
4. Draw a house or outdoor scene in ink. Cut a frisket to cover the illustration area, and create a graded wash in the sky area, grading from dark to light as you approach the horizon.

SUGGESTED PORTFOLIO PROJECTS

1. Try these approaches to incorporating transparent wash into your illustrations of simple accessories (such as handbags, gloves, or shoes):

   a. After drawing the accessory as an outline using pen-and-ink, paint a background of flat wash that creates a window around the subject.

   b. Set the accessory in a strong directional light, and create a light pencil outline, indicating changes in light and shade, on illustration board. Apply flat and graded washes that describe the object without outlining the various planes of the form. Add details to the finished drawing in ink.

   c. Draw the accessory as an outline in ink. Apply washes sparingly to emphasize particular details.

2. For an article promoting an active life, find or draw a figure in three related poses. First make thumbnail sketches of various arrangements, then create a silhouette outline of each. Transfer each outline to watercolor paper or illustration board. Complete the figures as silhouettes, using flat and graded transparent washes and no line work.

3. For an article on pet care, try the approach in project 2, using an animal as a model.

4. Use high-contrast silhouette or mapping to illustrate a figure in an active pose. Break the form into two or three values (light, medium, and dark) having distinct borders. Make a rough study from your source material, and transfer an outline sketch to airbrush paper, simplifying and stylizing the shadows so that their shapes are not only descriptive but interesting. Apply frisket, and cut along the lines of each defined shape. Finish the illustration using flat and graded airbrush washes.

5. Create an airbrushed illustration suitable for an advertisement for seaside vacations, such as a figure water-skiing; a collection of sunglasses, beach towel, and beach chair; or a sailboat. Simplify and stylize your subject to create impact.

6. Choose a complex subject, such as a motorcycle, sewing machine, or bicycle, and execute a product illustration that incorporates ink line with other techniques, such as watercolor wash, gouache, and/or airbrush. Employ each technique as creatively as possible to communicate the nature of your subject.

CHAPTER 6

COMPUTER ILLUSTRATION

Figure 6-1. *Hand Inserting Disk*, from a series of over 120 illustrations for a reference manual aimed at novice computer users. The artist created several drawings of various views and modified them for each instructional image. In this illustration, for example, a single key was rendered for the keyboard; the others were duplicated from the original and adjusted to fit. Creating this much detail using traditional inking techniques would have been both time-consuming and monotonous to execute. With the computer, this project was completed at 10 percent of the projected cost of using photographs. Media: Macintosh computer, Illustrator88. Output: Linotronic. (Illustrator: Steve Gorney)

G enerating artwork on a computer presents different options for artists and their clients than art produced with traditional media. The creative process, from conception to final alterations, may be faster and more cost-effective, or it may take longer but offer a greater variety of solutions. The computer can provide special effects, textures, and patterns that are difficult to create with other tools (figs. 6-1, 6-2). Additionally several programs can set up artwork for reproduction by appending registration marks and other instructions. Computer art can also be imported directly into printed materials and cropped or resized with ease. For these reasons many commercial studios prefer computer art.

Using a computer to make art first requires learning about, and putting your hands on, a computer. As with any graphics medium, you must acquire the knowledge and skills needed to make this technology work for you, and mastery is the result of diligent effort and practice. But it is, after all, the message of your illustration, not

J. Gikow 88

Figure 6-2. This floral illustration used for self-promotional purposes was drawn in Illustrator88. Objects, such as the vase and each leaf arrangement, were each drawn on individual layers and positioned as desired. A special pattern-generating tool was used to create the wallpaper pattern. Output: Laser printer. (Illustrator: Jacqueline Gikow)

the technology, that matters, so you should also understand the traditional techniques of communication in print.

Nothing in electronic graphics is too technical or mysterious for you to learn on your own. Although a computer system can process and deliver information at high speed, it is not an intelligent being; it functions only when you give it the proper commands. If you understand this, then enthusiasm, a set of goals, and time set aside to practice are the only requirements for moving from intimidation to mastery (fig. 6-3).

COMPUTER GRAPHICS TECHNOLOGY

The first computers were big, cumbersome, and expensive, and people using them had to learn complicated instructions called programming languages. This meant that graphics created on the first computers were more often executed by scientists or computer engineers than by artists. As technology improved, computers became smaller and more accessible, and artists with a technical bent began to experiment with them. Further miniaturization of computer technology resulted in independent personal computers, which increased the units' efficiency and the users' control over them. The technology continues to develop at a fast pace, and the applications programs are getting easier to use.

You can now create pictures with almost any personal computer, but the system that made relatively inexpensive detailed black-and-white illustration possible for artists was the Macintosh. Introduced in 1984, the Macintosh revolutionized the personal computer industry—with its user-friendly interface. Apple standardized and promoted among software developers a way for the user to interact intuitively with the computer through the use of familiar pictorial images called *pictograms* or *icons*. Then the PostScript programming language, which was capable of directing a laser printer to produce finely detailed images, established the Mac as a serious tool for black-and-white illustration.

Today the IBM PC, Amiga, and many other computers capable of taking advantage of better resource output devices, are also firing the imagination of both artists and illustrators (fig. 6-4).

Some of these systems are simple to operate, requiring very little specialized knowledge; others are complex and require extensive training. If you want to work with many systems you will need a broad understanding of basic computer principles. To operate one or two systems, you may get by with only functional knowledge of those particular systems, although understanding com-

Figure 6-3. *Appeal*, student illustration using the Apple II computer. Shown are three versions of the same basic image. (Illustrator: Catherine Tower)

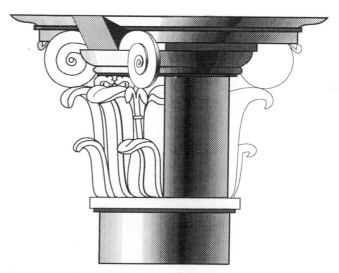

Figure 6-4. Architectural detail of a Corinthian capital drawn on the IBM PC using Arts & Letters, drawing program. A PostScript gradient was used to create the shading. (Illustrator: Maureen Jones)

plex systems sometimes requires extensive training. Since the operating specifics vary widely from computer to computer, as well as between software packages, refer to the literature that accompanies your equipment to find out how best to use it. If your interest in computer-generated graphics grows, look into the many books that discuss advanced hardware, software, techniques, and media in full detail.

BASIC COMPUTER WORKSTATION

To create art on a computer you need a workstation that includes some basic equipment.

Hardware. As the name implies, hardware includes the physically tangible parts of your system.

The *system unit* includes the *central processing unit* (CPU), which is the computer's brain. The CPU does most of the work, performing mathematical calculations necessary to translate your graphics instructions into pictures. It also holds the memory. To store graphics and data while working with graphics, you need a CPU with at least one megabyte of random access memory (RAM).

To the system unit you attach the *keyboard*, a *monitor* (a video screen), and a mouse or graphics tablet and stylus—all devices that send your drawing motions to the CPU for interpretation. You will probably need a *hard disk*. This is a storage device, which will hold your graphic programs and the work you save. Although you can also use a floppy disk drive for smaller, fairly limited programs, more sophisticated—and more rewarding—graphics programs require a hard disk. The hard disk can either be external (a box that sits beside the computer), or internal (the memory comes on electronic components that are attached inside the computer).

A very handy input device for the commercial studio or the experienced user is a *digitizing device*, such as a camera or scanner. These put a photograph or drawn or painted image into the computer's memory, making it available for manipulation or incorporation into your image (fig. 6-5). Some artists prefer working up fairly complete images in conventional media, then digitizing them for further development with the computer.

Regardless of the differences in computer programs, the computer handles artwork of any type in the same way: the image seen on the monitor screen is made up of dots. Each dot is a *picture element*, or *pixel*, and the screen image consists of a collection of these dots turned on or off as the picture is developed. The resolution

Figure 6-5. Student illustration using the scanned images of a face. The image was stretched and compressed vertically and horizontally in a series of repeats, using the original high-contrast black and various patterns. The base of the tree was executed with a paint program. (Illustrator: Mary Fraser)

Figure 6-6. Student illustration using Fullpaint, a Macintosh paint program. (Illustrator: Mark Austin)

Figure 6-7. *Paint Tube*, one of a series of art supply illustrations drawn in Image Studio, and then used to produce an animated video. Output: Laser print. (Illustrator: Diane Margolin)

(number of pixels per linear inch) differs from system to system. Most artists prefer working with the higher resolution systems, which allow more detail.

Eventually you will want to *output* your finished image as *hard copy*, a stable form of the image that can be carried away from the computer. The most popular output device by far for black-and-white artwork is the printer. The program and the printer you use determine the look of the printed illustration. The three types of printers useful for black-and-white computer art are the *dot-matrix*, the *ink jet*, and the *laser printer*. These differ according to the number and size of dots they print per inch as well as the printer's ability to read programming languages. For example, a PostScript printer can output what you see on a monitor at 72 dots per inch (DPI), as 300 DPI or more.

Software. The two generic types of graphic art on the computer are "Paint," or bit-mapped, graphics; and "Draw," or object-oriented, vector graphics.

Paint programs treat the entire screen as a collection of dots. Mimicking traditional drawing and painting techniques, a paint program allows you to create images by turning individual pixels on or off using "pencils," "erasers," and "paintbrushes" (fig. 6-6). Visually the pixels collectively create the image. A computer painting is called a bit-mapped image because at least one bit (the smallest amount of memory) is assigned to each pixel, and the pixels are arranged in a rectangular matrix. Each pixel has its own "address" and information and is independent of other pixels. In a bit-mapped image the software does not recognize what the pixels represent—it cannot distinguish between an ear and a plant, for instance. It only discerns whether the bits are turned on or off. Turning off or on these pixels makes a mark on the screen in much the same way as drawing on a pad or canvas (fig. 6-7). For this reason, the monitor-mouse or -tablet situation is called an electronic canvas.

Drawing programs produce object-oriented, or vector, graphics. Using "drafting" tools such as straightedges, rulers, and templates, you work with a range of geometric shapes, called primitives. These include lines, curves, circles, rectangles, etc. They are combined to form the image in the same way a technical illustrator uses ellipse guides and triangles to draw. Each shape, however, is recognized by the computer as a separate object (hence "object-oriented"). Each object retains its shape, size, visual texture, and boundary as though it were drawn on a separate sheet of clear acetate, and the acetate sheets layered to form the image. You can move shapes around independently, even slide them behind or in front of the other objects in a drawing (fig. 6-8).

The output resolution and flexibility of black-and-white computer artwork leaped forward with the introduction of PostScript, a programming language—or set of instructions—capable of producing high resolution and finely detailed output. Delicate, complicated patterns and gradients, gradual transitions from any percentage of black to another percentage, were made easy by PostScript (figs. 6-9, 6-10). Because PostScript is copyrighted, other languages that will produce similar effects are under development.

Figure 6-8. *Sunburn Explainer,* created in MacDraw and used in an article about the effects of the sun on skin. Output: Laser print. (© Copyright 1989, Knight-Ridder Tribune News/Bill Baker)

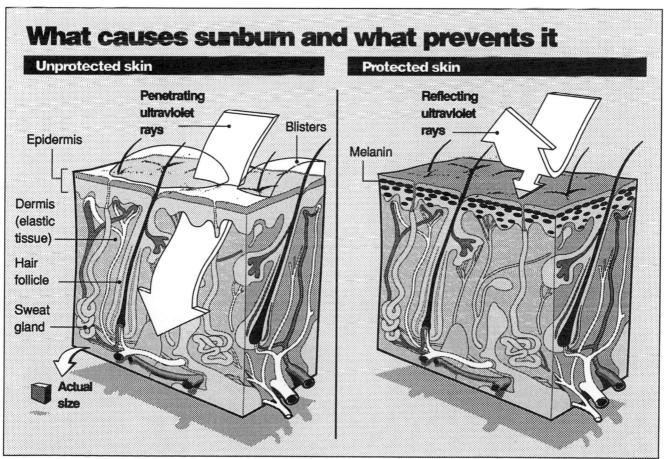

Figure 6-9. Illustration used as signage for a shopping center. A blueprint elevation was scanned to act as a template in Illustrator88, an elevation was developed by tracing over the template, and finally, the elevations were skewed to create an isometric drawing. Output: Linotronic. (Illustrator: Michael Crumpton, Building designs: Graham Gund Architects)

Figure 6-10. Logo for River Park Nursery School. Created in FreeHand, which allows special effects such as curving the type around the illustration. Output: Linotronic. (Illustrator: Steve Gorney)

Whether you develop skills on the Mac, the IBM PC, Amiga, or other computer, art produced by computer is like any other area of the illustration field. Like pencils, airbrushes, and other drawing tools, computers do not generate work by themselves. Any computer-generated art is the result of the illustrator's talent, skill, experience, and knowledge of software (figs. 6-11, 6-12).

Figure 6-11. Student illustration. Scanned image combined with the paint program, Fullpaint. (Illustrator: Phil Doney)

Figure 6-12. *Packing a Lot of Punches*, test illustration using CorelDRAW with PostScript patterns. What the illustrator sees on the screen is a visual code denoting the pattern, which is usually printed in an accessory book because it is too complicated for the resolution available on the monitor. (Illustrator: Maureen Jones)

CHAPTER 7

ILLUSTRATION MARKETS

Timber Wolf (Canis lupus), an illustration for a collection of poetry. Media: Ink on scratchboard. (Illustrator: Trudy Nicholson. From *Scratchboard* by Ruth Lozner. Watson-Guptill, 1990.)

n addition to imagery, medium, technique, and style, black-and-white illustration can be categorized by the market for which it is prepared. Advertising and editorial illustration are the two major types; a number of specialized areas also require black-and-white illustration.

ADVERTISING

Advertising consists largely of image creation, because the success of a product often depends on how the manufacturer presents it to the public. The image presented in a print advertisement, often some sort of pictorial representation combined with typography, must perform several functions: announce the existence of a product, draw attention to it, and emphasize its desirable qualities. Illustration is a vital part of this message from the manufacturer to the consumer.

Each step of an advertising campaign is carefully

planned and evaluated, and a number of people play roles in the generation of concepts for illustration. The client provides basic requirements for the presentation of the product. The designer or art director, usually working with a copy writer, devises the promotional concept and commissions an illustrator, either directly or through an agent. The illustrator then translates the concept outlined by an art director on behalf of the client, perhaps through the directives of the agent, with the intention of reaching a targeted audience.

To convey information, advertisers often use realistic illustrations. Sales of cars, clothes, and furniture, for instance, depend on appearance. Ads for technical products, such as tools or machines, must show functional details. To create an accurate representation, you need either the product or a photograph of it before you begin (fig. 7-1). Tracing or transferring from a photo, using one of the techniques described in chapter 2, will provide you with correct proportions.

In some cases you must interpret rather than simply depict the subject, whether it is tangible (a sofa) or intangible (the environment of a hotel). An assignment may require your work to be more precise than a photograph or to include details that would not show in one. You may depict a product being used, show the results, or exaggerate the usefulness (or the attractiveness) of the product to distinguish it from the competition. You might combine realism with fantasy to set a mood or to

Figure 7-1. Realistic product illustrations that depict functional details, used in mail-order catalogs and newspaper advertising. Medium: Pen-and-ink. (Illustrator: Joseph Schweizer)

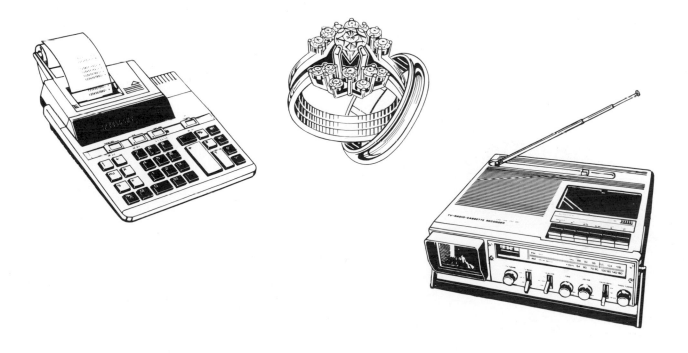

Figure 7-2. *Call-A-Holic*, for a telephone company advertising the benefits of having an extra phone line in your home. The artist was given the headline and a general idea of the visuals that the art director wanted. He used his own home kitchen as reference for the setting of this illustration. Media: Pen-and-ink, watercolor overlay. (Illustrator: Bill Mayer)

Figure 7-3. *Fragrance Imitators*, from a magazine article about counterfeit perfumes. A tight deadline made the use of collage a practical choice for this illustration. Media: Collage, watercolor, chalk on black illustration board. (Illustrator: Doris Ettlinger)

create an environment that enhances the product's appeal (fig. 7-2). When there is no tangible product to portray, you might illustrate an idea or provide a positive image for your client.

EDITORIAL

As newspapers and magazines proliferated in the nineteenth century, editorial illustration became a viable market. Often eclipsed by photography during the twentieth century, it remains a good source of employment, a showcase for new talent, and a place for experienced illustrators to try different styles and techniques. Fees are traditionally lower for editorial illustration than for advertising, but illustrators like the editorial side for the variety it provides (fig. 7-3). One assignment might be for the cover of a trade magazine; a second for a newspaper article on environmental changes; a third for a consumer magazine feature about nutritional concerns of the family in a two-career household.

An illustrator looking for editorial work meets with the publication's art director, and the communication between illustrator and art director is more direct than in advertising. Editorial illustrators usually receive more interpretative freedom than illustrators in other markets (fig. 7-4).

SPECIAL MARKETS

Specialized illustrations, which require more than basic drawing ability, serve several purposes. They show things that cannot be photographed. They demonstrate how things work. And they focus the viewer's attention by exaggerating, enhancing, and labeling important parts, or by eliminating unnecessary details. There are four categories of specialized illustration: technical, scientific, fashion, and children's book illustration.

Technical Illustration. Technical illustration involves translating information from industry, architecture, engineering, and business into pictures that people who are not specialists can understand. This artwork appears in how-to manuals, textbooks, professional and reference publications, special-interest magazines, and museum and trade show exhibitions.

Success depends upon the artist's ability to present the subject, be it facts and figures or aspects of a product or process, clearly and precisely, using interesting visual forms. These may include exterior views that show overall appearance; exploded drawings that explain the relationship of parts; cutaways and cross sec-

Figure 7-4. *Japanese Garden*, from a newspaper article on gardening. In order to create an effective black-and-white sculptural image, the illustrator used the natural textures of the paper for contrast. Medium: Paper sculpture. (Illustrator: Lisa Tysko)

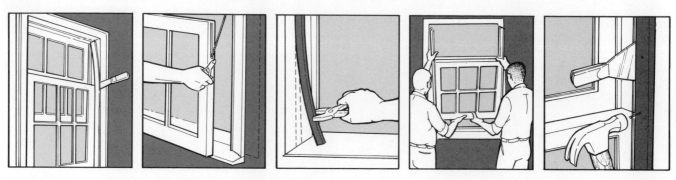

Figure 7-5. *How to Install Window Channels*, from a newspaper article on home repairs. Medium: Pen-and-ink. (Illustrator: Edward Lipinski)

Figure 7-6. *Lowell V Photo Lamp*, a catalog illustration. The actual lamp was supplied, and the artist took it apart to understand how to create an exploded view. Media: Macintosh computer using Illustrator88. (Illustrator: Michael Crumpton)

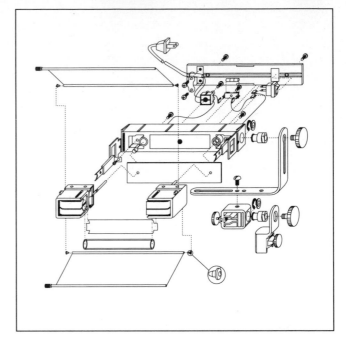

tions that provide details of components normally concealed; and diagrams that show electrical or mechanical functions. As figures 7-5 and 7-6 show, a technical illustrator should understand how things work. Some background in drafting and math, an understanding of perspective, and the ability to interpret blueprints or plan drawings are helpful, along with a good working knowledge of graphic design and typography.

Information Graphics. Information graphics, a form of technical illustration, can communicate both quantitative and qualitative information. Quantitative information consists of data that can be counted or measured and is usually presented in abstract, two- or three-dimensional bar graphs, line graphs, pie diagrams, or tables. Presenting quantitative information in a less abstract, more pictorial form involves finding an image that both conveys the data and reflects its meaning (fig. 7-7). Qualitative information describes the characteristics of its subject. More concerned with explanations, it

Figure 7-7. *Savings and Loan Bailout.* Illustration for a newspaper editorial based on statistical information supplied by the editor. The illustrator presented the quantitative information in pictorial form and had the editor's permission to loosely interpret the data. The illustrator was chosen because his style and medium allowed him to meet the short (24 hour) deadline. Media: Ink on scratchboard. (Illustrator: Robert Zimmerman)

$1 billion
If $1 billion were put in one-year certificates of deposit, the interest after a year would be about $80 million.

$1.3 billion
What it cost Donald Trump to build the Taj Mahal hotel and casino

$5 billion
What Apple Computer is worth, as valued by the stock market

$10 billion
Anheuser-Busch's value on the stock market.

$100 billion
Gross national product of Saudi Arabia.

$300 billion
U.S. defense spending for 1989.

$325 billion
General Accounting Offices's estimate of savings and loan bailout's cost.

$500 billion
G.A.O.'s pessimistic estimate (According to an even gloomier forecast in the Stanford Law and Policy Review, the total could go to $1.4 trillion.)

appears as flow charts, chronological charts, relationship charts, and maps, all of which lend themselves to creative interpretation (figs. 7-8, 7-9).

Consider the nature of the information and the audience when designing a diagram of any sort. The purpose of these illustrations is to make the information clear, useful, and attractive to the viewer. For example, maps of urban transit systems are usually abstract, with routes and connections simplified into clean graphic symbols. Hierarchy charts call for a combination of abstract imagery and typography. Diagrams of natural or industrial processes communicate best with pictures.

Beware of misrepresenting quantitative data in service of an eye-catching visual. You may repeat images to show quantity; however, you must adjust the image's width as well as its height to depict percentages accu-

How a Forest Recycles Water

Figure 7-8. *How a Forest Recycles Water*, from a newspaper article on environmental issues. Because of a tight deadline requirement, last-minute changes to this illustration had to be done on site at the time of submission. Media: Pen-and-ink, airbrush. (Illustrator: Edward Lipinski)

Figure 7-9. *Cross-country Riding Competition*, for British television guide explaining a cross-country riding course. The illustrator wanted to show the severity of some of the obstacles confronting the horses and distinguish the living horse and rider from the arduous man-made obstacle course. He used graduated tint screens to make the animals more "photographic" and left the obstacles more diagrammatic. Media: Pen-and-ink, Letratone screens. (Illustrator: Nigel Holmes)

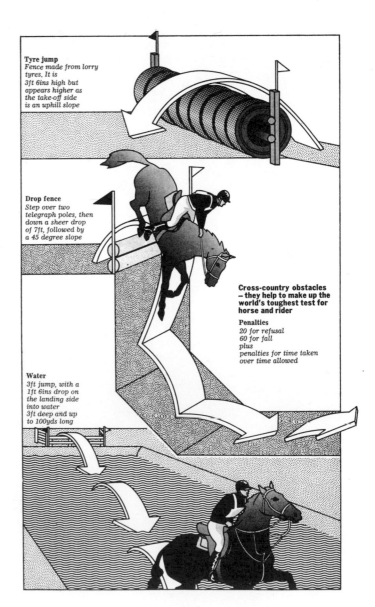

Figure 7-10. *View of Courtyard*, an architectural perspective for the Federal Triangle Competition, Washington, D.C. The beaux-arts watercolor wash technique that the artist used helps the proposed structure fit with the existing architecture. Medium: Ivory black watercolor wash. (Illustrator: Thomas Schaller; architects: Kohn Pedersen Fox Associates, P.C.)

rately. Pictorial accuracy in qualitative charts and maps may be left to your discretion. If you remain aware of the responsibility of accurately conveying information, you will find that creative opportunities abound. Illustrating information is an area that is in increasing demand.

Architectural Illustration. Architectural illustration can be quick sketches, presentation drawings, or elaborate promotional pieces. These categories are loosely defined, and illustrations often serve several purposes (fig. 7-10).

Preliminary sketches are valuable aids in conceptualizing architectural projects. For sketching, good freehand skills serve as well as formal techniques, but the artist must follow the rules of composition, perspective, and scale. Sketch materials usually include soft lead pencils, charcoal, felt-tip markers, and tracing paper.

After completion of the planning stage, the illustrator, perhaps working with designers, develops a presentation drawing. Working from blueprints, the artist renders a building or interior as it will look after construction. Architectural illustrators often come out of

Figure 7-11. A preliminary sketch showing one residence concept. Medium: Pencil. (Illustrator/architect: Paul Stevenson Oles, FAIA)

design programs with courses in drafting, drawing, and interpreting blueprints. Artists must be able to render the different material used in construction (glass, wood, metal, cement, brick, plastic, tile) and landscaping (grass, shrubs, plants, trees), as well as to draw figures to scale. Illustration media include pen-and-ink, watercolor wash, gouache, airbrush, and combinations of these (figs. 7-11, 7-12, 7-13).

Advertising agencies use architectural illustrations in brochures and print ads. A typical brochure might feature drawings of the models for each unit in a development, floor plans, and vignettes of architectural details. Ads placed in periodicals often include adaptations of the original drawing, combining the architecture with a recreational activity, for instance, to convey ambience.

Scientific Illustration. Produced as a visual aid for both professionals and nonprofessionals, scientific illustration communicates information from the natural science and medical fields. Although serious and fac-

Figure 7-12. A computer-generated illustration showing design development, indicating the steep terrain as a series of steps. (Illustrator/architect: Paul Stevenson Oles, FAIA)

Figure 7-13. The finished rendering of the residence, shown situated in a photograph of the actual site. The photograph was taken from the specific point of the perspective drawing, at a time that would correspond to the shadows in the rendering. The drawing was then pasted down onto the photograph. Medium: Black Prismacolor pencil. (Illustrator/architect: Paul Stevenson Oles, FAIA)

tual, it need not be dry or monotonous. In fact, illustrations should be eye-catching and as up to date as the content, perhaps combining traditional and computer techniques.

Scientists and virtually all scientific publications prefer black-to-white illustrations because of their clarity when reproduced (fig. 7-14). Specialization in black-and-white does not limit you to outlines and flat images, however. Line drawings in pen-and-ink, which lowers production costs, may include crosshatching and stipple techniques. Tonal drawings in pencil, watercolor, carbon dust, and charcoal allow for delicate value indications and easy-to-read reproduction.

Natural science refers to the study of civilization past and present, all living creatures, the ground on which we stand, and the matter from which we are constructed. Major areas include anthropology, paleontology, biology, geology, botany, and zoology, each of which is further subdivided. Because of this diversity, an illustrator working in the natural sciences may take a broad or a narrow focus. A thorough knowledge of scientific terminology is not required, although a general knowledge of biology and human anatomy will be a great help (fig. 7-15).

Drawing from nature—sketching flora and fauna—is not scientific illustration unless the illustration accurately represents scientific data or factual material. While natural science illustration leaves room for individual style, accuracy is vital. All facets of the subject,

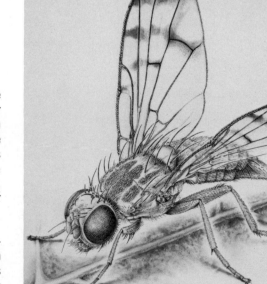

Figure 7-14. Fruit fly *(Neaspilota vernoniae)* on leaf, used as a frontispiece for a taxonomic research publication on a genus of fruit flies. Reference for the fly was a dry pinned specimen viewed through a microscope and a rough sketch of anatomic parts of the fly. The leaf was drawn in proportion to the magnification of the fly. Media: Carbon dust and diluted ink on 00 Ross board. (Illustrator: Elaine R. S. Hodges. From "Studies of Tereliinae (Diptera: Tephritidae): A Revision of the Genus *Neaspilota* Osten Saken," by Wayne N. Mathis and Amnon Freidberg, *Smithsonian Contributions to Zoology,* Number 439, 1986)

Figure 7-15. *Golden Lion Tamarins* was drawn from sketches and photographs the artist took at the National Zoo in Washington, D.C. The Brazilian rain-forest background was drawn from source photographs. Detailed textures in this scratchboard illustration enhance its drama and action. Media: Ink on scratchboard. (Illustrator: Trudy Nicholson. From *The Guild Handbook of Scientific Illustration,* Elaine R.S. Hodges, ed. Van Nostrand Reinhold, 1989.)

such as habitat, season, age of specimen, and even lighting, are not subject to interpretation.

Medical illustration is a highly specialized area of scientific illustration focusing on the human body (fig. 7-16). This work would appeal to someone who is attracted to both art and science. It demands a depth of knowledge best learned in a graduate medical illustration program, as well as an ability to draw with extreme accuracy and realism and to reduce complex ideas to simple explanatory diagrams or schematic concepts. A typical graduate program for medical illustration in-

Figure 7-16. Plating techniques for facial fractures, published in an atlas on cranial surgery. This illustration shows how reconstructive hardware is employed in a medical procedure prior to plastic surgery. Medium: Carbon dust. (Illustrator: Carmella Clifford)

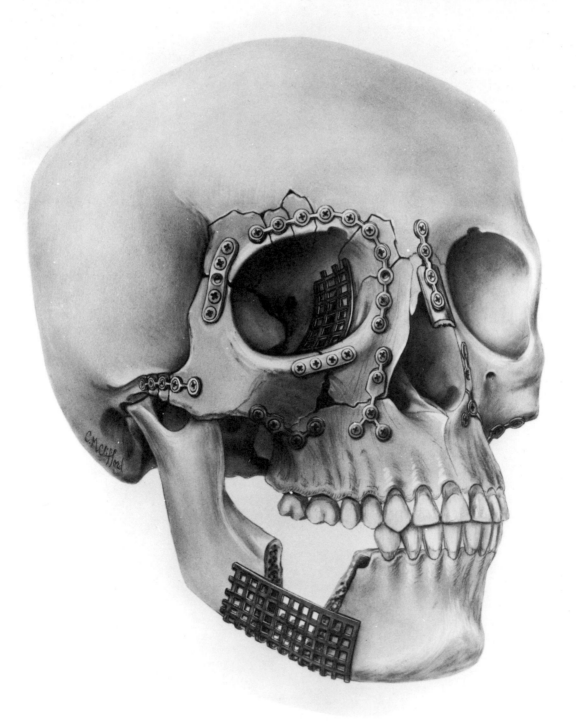

cludes courses in anatomy, pathology (study of disease), histology (microscopic study of cells), human physiology, human embryology, and neuroanatomy (the anatomy of the nervous system), as well as art and design.

Because the artist must rigorously adhere to established facts, medical illustration is often described as noncreative, even though it involves finding a format suitable for communicating those facts. For example, in recording a surgical procedure, the illustrator might create a three-dimensional visualization, differentiating and enhancing vital parts while eliminating unnecessary ones (such as the surgeon's hands, blood, towels, instruments). A photographic recording on the other hand, while both accurate and truthful, would be virtually unintelligible in this instance.

Fashion Illustration. Fashion illustration employs exaggeration and fantasy to create a successful image. The illustrator must know how clothing enhances the body, what the current beauty ideals are, and which style details should be omitted or exaggerated. Good fashion illustration encourages customers to envision themselves wearing the garment depicted.

Fashion illustrators often create the image of a fashionable product than rather than simply drawing a garment. The type of apparel and how the illustration will be used will influence the drawing style. An advertisement for a particular garment may be more realistically rendered than a sketch making a fashion statement about the garment, its designer, or a store that stocks it (fig. 7-17).

A fashion illustrator may draw from a live model or from a photograph provided by the client. Sometimes the illustrator only has the garment and must rely on an understanding of anatomy and clothing construction to create the model's pose and adapt the outfit to the figure's body. In any case, the basis of an illustration should be whatever best displays the garment. The artist might choose to exaggerate a curve, line, or texture; the model's posture or attitude; or characteristics such as height, shoulder width, body shape, or hairstyle. Including decorative objects, such as flowers, drawing a background scene, such as a landscape or city street, or showing action, such as running or jumping, can help to create an appropriate mood.

Drawing Proportions and Figure Guidelines. The current ideal figure for women's fashions is young, athletic, tall, and slender, far different from the shorter and heavier proportions of most women's bodies. The idealized woman has a small bosom and broad shoulders and wears a size six, eight, or ten. Total body length is eight

Figure 7-17. This illustration employed a bold, graphic approach to promote a fashion show. It was used as a program cover and as a poster. Medium: Pantone marker. (Illustrator: Kathi M. Kerr)

times the length of the head (fig. 7-18), with neck and legs elongated to retain fairly realistic proportions. More sophisticated drawings use figures up to ten heads high, perhaps wearing high-heeled shoes. Hair and makeup range from natural to stylized, depending on the clothing showcased.

The male fashion figure is usually less exaggerated than the female. He has a slim torso with a well-defined neck, shoulders, and muscle structure. Men's fashions change more slowly and subtly than women's, so an illustrator must concentrate primarily on attention to details and small variations in style and fabric (fig. 7-19).

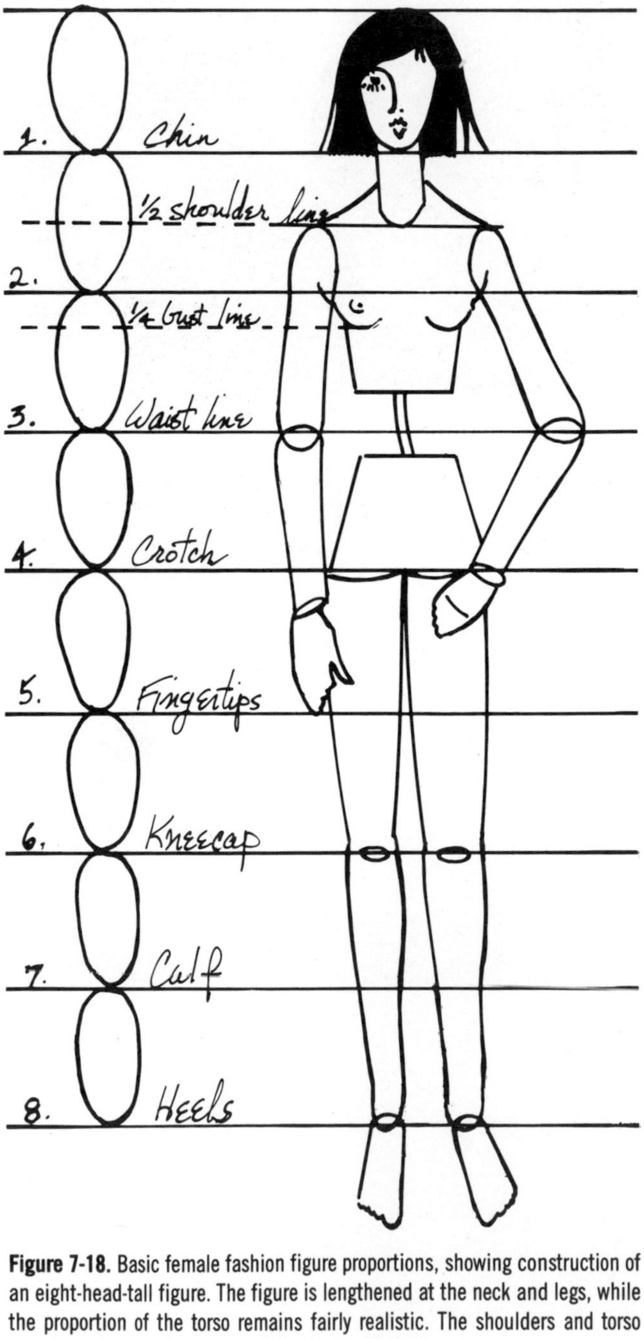

1. Chin
   ½ shoulder line
2.
   ¼ bust line
3. Waist line
4. Crotch
5. Fingertips
6. Kneecap
7. Calf
8. Heels

Figure 7-18. Basic female fashion figure proportions, showing construction of an eight-head-tall figure. The figure is lengthened at the neck and legs, while the proportion of the torso remains fairly realistic. The shoulders and torso are also narrower than those of the average woman.

Figure 7-19. Unpublished fashion illustration of a male. Media: Charcoal, charcoal pencil. (Illustrator: Thea Kliros)

Children's body proportions differ radically from adult proportions; each age has inherent figure problems that require special design solutions. The toddler's head, for instance, is about one-fourth of the total body length. As the child grows, the head becomes smaller in proportion to the lengthening body. In general, fashion children should look slender and active, well fed but not plump (fig. 7-20).

The face—a focal point—gives a fashion illustration definition and character. Features should be balanced symmetrically and establish age without being overly defined. The head is oval shaped, fuller at the forehead. Placed at the midline of the head, eyes are almond shaped and spaced one eye-length apart.

Children's Book Illustration. Through the illustrations in children's books, young people can experience new worlds. Real or imaginary, these places may be filled with all sorts of creatures doing and expressing all sorts of things (fig. 7-21). Seeing them, children can learn to understand their own environments and to identify their own emotions. Illustrations lead them into reading by creating a representation of the written descriptions and may also help them to develop a sense of aesthetics.

Picture storybooks focus attention and stimulate creative thinking in youngsters. Given a book about a duck visiting a variety of farm animals, a one-year-old might learn to name the animals, while a three-year-old might imagine conversations between them. The creative possibilities of this format are attractive to artists, but the picture book is only one way to reach a juvenile audience.

Books designed for learning to read need illustrations that show action in a lively manner. Books aimed at older children require illustrations that are usually realistic and quite detailed (fig. 7-22). Educational publishing may offer some opportunities for beginning artists as well as those who are more established.

An illustrator of children's books faces a unique challenge in communicating to young readers by combining fine and graphic arts skills. Even if you have had broad art training, chances are that you have not focused on subjects common to children's books or on developing a style to which children will relate. Drawing people or animals in a variety of poses while retaining a convincing consistency of character is not easy. Ruth Shedrofsky's portfolio samples of adolescent girls in figures 7-23 and 7-24 help an art buyer visualize her ability to depict a character in a consistent manner. A warm, personal touch is essential. Children of all ages

Figure 7-20. Illustration of children to promote seasonal patterns and textures for a fabric company. Medium: Charcoal. (Illustrator: Thea Kliros)

Figure 7-21. Illustration for a children's coloring book called *The Nutcracker and the Mouse King*. Resource material for this illustration included historical books on fashion. Medium: Pen-and-ink. (Illustrator: Thea Kliros)

Figure 7-22. *Waitin' for the Day*, for a story from the book *Jump On Over!* on the adventures of Brer Rabbit and his family. Medium: Transparent watercolor. (Illustrator: Barry Moser, © Pennyroyal Press, Inc.)

Figure 7-23. *Three Girls Sharing a Secret*, a portfolio sample of children's book illustration. Medium: Pencil. (Illustrator: Ruth Shedrofsky)

Figure 7-24. *Back of a Car*. Three girls in a second pose for a portfolio. Medium: Pencil. (Illustrator: Ruth Shedrofsky)

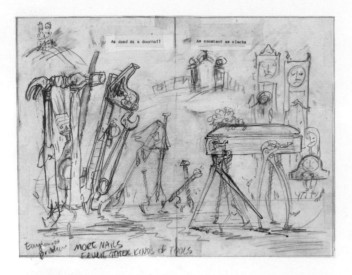

Figure 7-25. Rough sketch for the two-page spread shown in figure 7-26. The notes are the result of discussions with the editor and author. Medium: Pencil. (Illustrator: David Small)

Figure 7-26. *As Dead as a Doornail/As Constant as Clocks*. The manuscript for this book arrived as 120 pages of completely unconnected rhyming similes. The illustrator developed the illustration sequences by literally cutting the manuscript apart and rearranging the similes. He brainstormed word associations until pictures began to form in his mind. Medium: Pen-and-ink. (Illustrator: David Small. From *As: A Surfeit of Similes*, by Norton Juster.)

respond to a fresh and positive outlook on the world and to a sense of wonder.

As an illustrator of children's books, you may work from a given text, or you may devise the concept and illustrations on your own (figs. 7-25, 7-26). Many artists use a storyboard to visualize scenes, a large sheet of drawing paper that is divided into enough squares to lay out an entire book.. The standard picture-book format has thirty-two pages, with twenty-eight pages allotted to the story. If you break the story into a seven-part visual sequence, then expand each part into four pages, organizing the drawings will be relatively easy.

Because abilities change with each age group, you need to understand the requirements of each audience. Very young children, for instance, including babies and toddlers, respond to simple, wordless images they can understand immediately. Children aged four to nine are learning to read, but they need lively illustrations to hold their interest. Older children, including young adults, look for vivid action, interesting characters, and a definite sense of place.

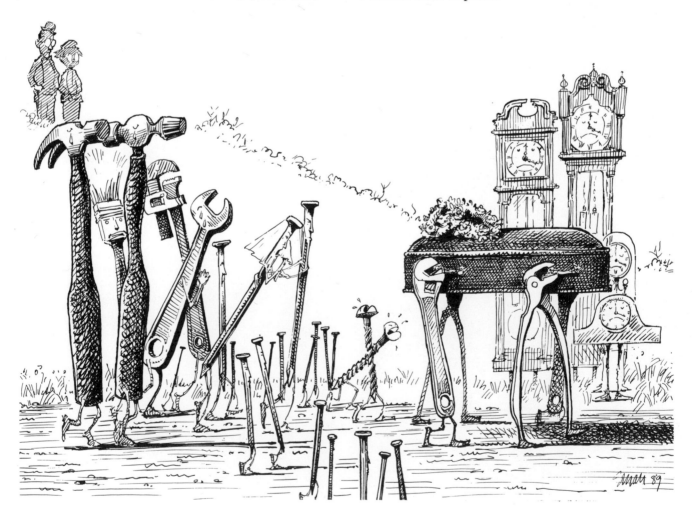

SUGGESTED PORTFOLIO PROJECTS

1. Realistically illustrate a product, such as furniture, shoes, or cosmetics, for a newspaper advertisement.

2. To advertise a health club, devise an interpretive illustration that shows the advantages of becoming a member.

3. Make a three- or four-step technical illustration that shows how to change a lightbulb, lace a shoe, or change a flat tire.

4. Illustrate a model home for a promotional brochure. Emphasize attractive details, such as bay windows, French doors, landscaping.

5. For a quantitative graph, find information on the amount of alcohol it takes to impair driving. Design a chart that illustrates the comparative effects of beer and hard liquor and shows the differences between critical quantities for men and women.

6. For an article on cooking with mushrooms, do a detailed illustration distinguishing four or five edible varieties.

7. Complete three fashion illustrations:
   a. Show realistic proportions, pattern design, and construction detail for a midpriced outfit.
   b. Create a highly stylized, gestural depiction of a high-fashion outfit; exaggerate the model's features.
   c. Depict a fantasy environment, either stylized or realistic, to promote a glamorous image.

8. For a wordless book aimed at toddlers, illustrate a nursery rhyme. Develop an eight-panel storyboard, then complete two panels in the medium and style of your choice.

9. For a book aimed at nine- to twelve-year-olds, create two illustrations showing a child doing household chores, such as cleaning the bedroom, helping with the dishes, or taking out the garbage. Use the same character for both drawings, but vary facial expressions and body positions.

10. Choose two chapters from an adventure story or romance aimed at teenagers, and illustrate the essential action of each.

CHAPTER 8

COMMUNICATION AND STYLE

Reverie of Vermeer, illustration for the title page of a book on scratchboard illustration. The inspiration for this illustration was Vermeer's painting, *The Geographer*. The illustrator translated Vermeer's technique to scratchboard and added details from a modern artist's studio. Media: Ink on scratchboard. (Illustrator: Ruth Lozner)

n illustration results from the partnership between a client and an illustrator, with success coming from the meeting of intent and interpretation. In other words, the visual image created by the artist reflects the concept and verbal description of the assignment provided by the client. The picture should help to clarify the words, make the subject matter concrete—in short, communicate.

Some illustrations literally illustrate a text, such as a rendering of a specific shoe for a shoe-store advertisement (fig. 8-1). Others go beyond literal meaning to evoke a feeling, to set a mood, or to coax the viewer into reading the text (fig. 8-2). Elements of the composition should work together to communicate the right message. When images reflect a variety of feelings, they themselves may tell the story, and the illustration may be enriched (fig. 8-3).

How you approach an illustration is as important as how you execute it. Effective communication, with a

Figure 8-1. Men's and women's watch illustrations, for an advertising campaign appearing primarily in newspapers. The artist took slides of the watches, which he then projected onto illustration board for inking. Media: Technical fountain pen, gouache. (Illustrator: Kevin Sprouls; © North American Watch Company)

Figure 8-2. *Crisis Game*, from a poster advertising a dramatic theater production about political games and the threat of war. The chessboard and a broken architectural artifact juxtaposed against civilian and military figures suggest the plot. Medium: Pen-and-ink. (Illustrator: Jacqueline Gikow)

Figure 8-3. Collage/montage illustration for an academic literary journal. Collage elements (depicting nature, history, the arts) relate man's role in the history of the state of Pennsylvania. Media: Graphite, watercolor dyes, gouache, ink, and applied collage elements. (Illustrator: Frederick H. Carlson)

client or with the client's audience, involves finding a common language. Become acquainted with the points of view of both before attempting to represent or reconcile them. Publications and advertisers have public images to develop and uphold. And their audience members share tastes, backgrounds, or experiences that may enable you to predict their responses to particular images. Just as two magazines with different viewpoints would present different articles on the same subject, your illustrations will take on different tones, straightforward or witty, simple or sophisticated, wholesome or risque, depending on the assignment. No fixed rules exist, unfortunately, to tell you exactly what message your work will convey, what feeling it will evoke in any given viewer. To reach the widest audience, you must search for imagery that anyone can understand. You must know what makes people laugh, look, think, what they fear and what they desire.

IMAGES AND SYMBOLS

No matter how abstract the concept, an illustration nearly always includes some recognizable form or figure. A recognizable, or realistic, drawing shows the distinctive characteristics of its subject, at times exaggerated, to make the image clear. Simple forms, such as a chair or an apple, can be conveyed by depicting their outer shape. Others, such as a ball of twine or a pillow, need added texture to be recognizable. The first step in planning a realistic drawing is to determine the essential physical qualities of the subject (fig. 8-4).

Your overall composition, the picture's underlying structure, consists of large abstract shapes that link the elements together and can also be arranged to communicate. Abstract form communicates on a more subtle level than recognizable images do, and they can strongly influence both the concept and mood of an illustration. For example, imagine an illustration showing three dolphins leaping out of the sea. One leaps to the left, its tail slightly above the water; the second leaps to the right, its tail underwater; the third, partly submerged, leaps slightly right of forward. This arrangement creates a large abstract shape, an inverted triangle, that will be a strong element in your illustration and can be used to develop drama. The composition consists of realistic images (the dolphins) and symbolic images (the triangular arrangement).

Images themselves become symbols, keys to communication, when they transcend the literal things that they represent. A heart symbolizes love or romance; a broken heart, lost love or great pain. A stretch limousine

Figure 8-4. Illustration for a corporate annual report. Two main shapes (man and heavy machinery) form the basis of a strong, simple, realistic composition. Medium: Pen-and-ink. (Illustrator: Chuck McVicker)

Figure 8-5. *The Future Is Now,* from a newspaper article on the fast pace of technology. Contrasting an old image symbolizing technology with a new one to convey both a fast pace and sophistication, the illustrator used a classic car as a spaceship flying through an urban landscape. Medium: Pen-and-ink. (Illustrator: Jacqueline Gikow)

symbolizes wealth; an antique car, nostalgia. A tiger symbolizes danger; a cat, domesticity. Of course, each of these images can take on countless other symbolic meanings, depending on factors such as the relationships among images, the context of the image, individual psychology, and cultural changes or developments (figs. 8-5, 8-6).

Imagine a mouse scampering through an open field. Now imagine a mouse scampering through a kitchen. The first description conjures up an image, perhaps playful and free, of wildlife. An animal in its natural environment searches for food, returns to its shelter, escapes from a predator: your sympathy is with the mouse. The second description changes the context so that you view the mouse not as wildlife but as vermin. The theme changes from freedom to cleanliness, and the situation (a creature out of place), rather than the subject, becomes the point of interest. In addition, the mood of either picture would change, by implication, with the introduction of a cat or a person with a carving knife.

The point here is that there is language of symbolism, and you can convey entirely different meanings by placing the same subject in two different settings. Images gain or lose meaning as you change the elements within and around them (fig. 8-7). Your choice of imagery and manipulation of context will determine the ability of an illustration to communicate clearly. If an image is not easily identified in its setting, the point of the story, the humor of the situation, the drama, can be lost.

You create ambiguous messages by presenting conflicting images; for example, an advertisement that places an expensive automobile in a rundown neighborhood would hardly stress the car's elegance. Images that have purely personal meanings also are ambiguous. Asked to illustrate an article on wildflowers, a student produced a drawing dominated by an assortment of roses and tulips, which as a rule are not wildflowers to the United States. The student explained that these flowers grew in a field behind the house she lived in as a child, so to her they symbolized wildness. But no one else would have understood the imagery.

Some images appear so often in the same symbolic context that they become tedious and no longer evoke a powerful response. Avoiding these insidious cliches can be difficult because you think of them immediately (the holiday turkey, a Valentine's Day heart) and because there is a fine line between a recognizable cultural symbol and a tired idea. Since you want your illustrations to

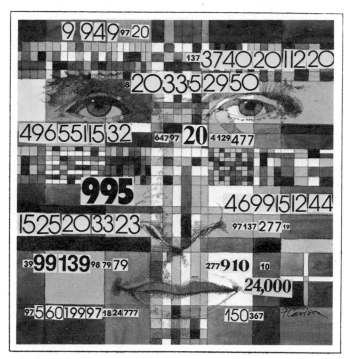

Figure 8-6. *No Memory*, from a magazine article about memorizing numbers. The subject's portrait is submerged in a grid, obscured by the maze of numbers he must recall. Collage elements are used to depersonalize the numbers the subject had to remember. Media: Graphite, dyes, collage. (Illustrator: Frederick H. Carlson)

Figure 8-7. *Refrigerator*, from a magazine article about writing a cookbook on chocolate. The concept depicts an overweight refrigerator, "fat" with chocolate. Media: Black Prisma pencil on coquille board. (Illustrator: Janice Belove)

Figure 8-8. Cliched images for holidays. (Source: Dover Clip-Art Series)

Figure 8-9. *Piece of the Pie*, for an article about federal laws requiring companies to use a certain percentage of minority suppliers. This artist transcends the cliche by an unusual use of money as a pie filling. This simple idea becomes even more interesting with the addition of shallow pictorial space, dynamic composition, and collage elements. Media: Watercolor with collage. (Illustrator: Doris Ettlinger)

draw on common experience, seek to use familiar images in a fresh way rather than rejecting them outright (figs. 8-8, 8-9).

Because a cultural symbol relates to the way of life of given people at a given time, symbolism is dynamic, changing as the world changes. Forty years ago an assembly line stood as a dominant image of technology. Today the computer represents that image updated. You can make certain assumptions about the way of life, and such institutions as school, work, and sports, in your time and place, and from these derive generally recognizable images.

MEANING

How do you draw meaning? Most illustrations communicate an idea through exaggeration (fig. 8-10). This does not mean distorting every image into a caricature but, rather, deliberately focusing on details to elicit the appropriate response (fig. 8-11). Response, emotional or intellectual, comes from identification, so your task as an illustrator is to match gesture and meaning. You have probably heard someone describe a car as "sexy," a vegetable as "tired," or a house as "friendly." The objects have not expressed emotions; a viewer has translated appearances into feelings. When you look at a wilted or droopy vegetable, it looks the way you feel when you are tired, and so you attribute the feeling to the vegetable (fig. 8-12). The best way to bring emotional dimension to your illustrations is through this process of association.

People's postures, movements, and facial expressions give clues to their emotional states. You must identify the physical characteristics that would be exhibited by a person feeling the emotion you seek to convey, then emphasize these traits to reinforce the feeling. You could, for instance, draw a person's hands clenched, wide open, or folded to portray, respectively, tension, excitement, or relaxation (fig. 8-13). Facial expressions convey a great range of emotions, from sadness (downturned mouth) to determination (gritted teeth), anger (scowl) to ecstasy (wide eyes), grief (tears) to joy (broad smile). Likewise, the position of the figure can set a mood: turning away can indicate secrecy or despair while facing forward can show openness or aggression.

To transfer human qualities to nonhuman subjects, similar attributes for each emotional state can be applied to the subject. For example, a healthy plant will have full leaves, open blossoms, and bursting buds; a dejected house will have a battered structure and windows in disrepair.

Figure 8-10. *Charles Manson—Media God*, a student illustration for an assignment on a series on crime. Both the media and the drawing style contribute to the lurid quality. Media: Graphite and dyes. (Illustrator: Greg Houston, Pratt Institute)

Figure 8-12. Illustration from a food and fitness newspaper column. The art director wanted a light-hearted, "fun" drawing. The artist's concept includes a frying pan that suggests a pool or lake, and vegetables that become the bathers. Media: Black Prisma pencil on coquille board. (Illustrator: Janice Belove)

Figure 8-11. Illustration from a newspaper article on the difference between fur and hair. The illustration builds humor by showing how an Afghan hound and its owner might look alike. Media: Black Prisma pencil on cold-press illustration board. (Illustrator: David Street; art director: Cindy Daniels)

Figure 8-13. *Are Your Operations out of Control?*, from a health-club magazine article on how a computer can ease the job of the club receptionist. For source material the artist shot about two dozen Polaroid pictures of hands and referred to an extensive reference file. Medium: Ebony pencil. (Illustrator: Kathleen Volp)

EXERCISES

1. Draw familiar objects (such as a chair, a hot dog, a hat) so that they are immediately recognizable by shape alone. Communicate the subject without creating an overly detailed illustration.
2. Draw familiar objects that need texture to be identified, such as a ball of yarn, a bath towel, a golf ball.
3. Create three images of a plant as it displays three distinct emotions, for instance, happiness, hunger, and sadness.
4. Draw images of three different figures, each displaying the same emotion, for example: a happy child, a happy hat, a happy owl; or an angry cloud, an angry celery stalk, an angry goldfish.
5. Draw two images displaying different emotions and interacting with one another, such as a tired car and an angry driver, or a curious cat and an inviting tree.

FANTASY

Many illustrations incorporate elements of fantasy to emphasize particular points. A distortion or rearrangement of reality adds symbolic meaning to an illustration by disrupting the viewer's expectations. Such images often appear in science fiction, children's books, humorous drawings, and political cartoons (figs. 8-14, 8-15, 8-16, 8-17).

Fantasy does not have to be complicated or disturbing, but it must include imagination and illusion. A subject might appear in an unnatural context (a banana peel opens to reveal a flower; a rabbit rides a bicycle). Sizes of objects might be reversed or the features exaggerated (a tiny person confronts a huge stack of dirty dishes; a greedy person is shown with an oversized hand). The subject could take on the identifying characteristics of another (a cloud takes on the shape of an elephant; vegetables have human facial features). The physical properties of an object could change (a rubber computer, a melting book). Such distortions depend upon an element of realism for impact. Carefully examine the visual possibilities of your assignment to determine if a fantastic element would suit your subject (fig. 8-18).

EXERCISES

1. Draw a subject in an unnatural context, for instance, a fish eating an ice-cream cone or a flower dancing on a stage.
2. Execute a portrait with exaggerated features, such as a small head on a normal body, or extralarge feet.
3. Combine the identifying characteristics of two subjects, such as a car and a horse or a rabbit and a human.
4. Change the physical properties (weight, density, or texture) of an object. You might depict a drooping clock or a transparent tree.

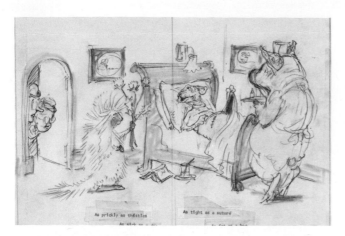

Figure 8-14. A two-page pencil sketch for the illustration shown in figure 8-15. Notice the changes and refinements that were made to both the characters and the background when the final illustration was developed. (Illustrator: David Small)

Figure 8-15. *As Prickly as Thistles*, a two-page spread from a children's book of similes. Medium: Pen-and-ink. (Illustrator: David Small. From *As: A Surfeit of Similes*, by Norton Juster.)

Figure 8-16 and 8-17. *More Rump* and *Say Cheeze*. These illustrations were for a series of small space ads appearing in a veterinary trade magazine. The client, an animal-feed supplier, asked for a humorous, unique style that would provide a consistent look during a year-long campaign. Media: Ink on scratchboard. (Illustrator: Bill Mayer)

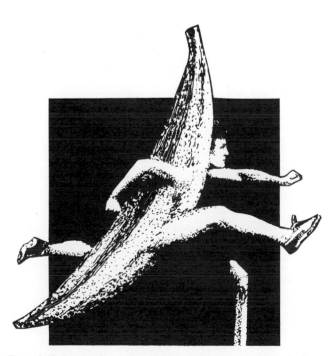

Figure 8-18. *Banana Races*, from a book on college trivia published by Peterson's. Medium: Pen-and-ink. (Illustrator: Douglas Rēinke)

ANALYZING THE SUBJECT

Outstanding illustrations tell the story accurately, and their underlying structure gives the message character and strength. Analyze the assignment to develop an effective approach to your subject.

Consider the assignment in general. What is the dominant idea? Can it be dramatized, or is it static? Can you tell the story in more than one way? What possibilities for emotional contrasts are there? How would you describe the subject (modern, antiquated, old, new, tawdry, wholesome, clean, rural, urban, unusual, average, inexpensive, costly)? How can you convey these characteristics?

Consider the components. Which figure is most important? What can you do to enhance each? What poses would each be likely to take? What do you know about their life-styles, cultures, backgrounds, habits, emotions? Is the situation dependent upon facial expressions? Should you add scenery, costumes, accessories?

Finally, consider the composition. Can you create a focal point with line, contrast, direction of gaze? Should the lighting be bright, dark, diffuse? Can you incorporate movement, pattern, geometric shapes, line, or informal subdivision?

STYLE

Style refers to the visual form that an illustrator gives to the subject matter: realistic, impressionistic, decorative, and so on. This may be a response to a particular subject, medium, or technique, or it may reflect the artist's personality. To understand the notion of stylistic variety, compare a single letter of the alphabet in different typefaces (fig. 8-19). Each figure conveys the same literal meaning, yet each makes a unique statement based on qualities of line, shape, and form. The personal treatment of subject matter by each illustrator sets each artist apart from the others. An art director will match an illustrator's personal style, or distinctive manner of expression, to a specific assignment in the same way that a designer chooses a typeface appropriate for a given text.

Elements of Style. The elements that make up the style of a picture work together to affect its reading. Flat, shallow, or deep pictorial space refers to the illusions of depth and volume developed through linear and atmospheric perspective (fig. 8-20). Composition, the underlying structure, may be symmetrical; static or

Figure 8-19. The letter *A* in four different typefaces—Helvetica, Times Roman, New Century Schoolbook, and Avant Garde.

Figure 8-20. *Diamond Head*, a portrait that started out as an intricately rendered illustration of a Hawaiian lei of human hair. In this example focus is directed toward the necklace without losing the importance of the face by extreme compression of the pictorial space. Medium: Pen-and-ink. (Illustrator: Ramsay)

Figure 8-21. *Home Poison Home*, from a magazine article of the dangers of insulation fumes. The physical structure of this composition is a square, but it is not a static square. The illustration is made dynamic by a variety of elements that break the edges, as well as by the interior space. Medium: Pen-and-ink. (Illustrator: Jacqueline Gikow)

dynamic; stable or active; horizontal, vertical, or diagonal (fig. 8-21). Representation is the manner, realistic or distorted, lively or stiff, in which subjects are depicted (fig. 8-22). Delineation is the quality of line, often dependent upon the tool or medium. It may be continuous or broken, heavy or light, soft or hard, descriptive or sketchy, bold or delicate, calligraphic or geometric (fig. 8-23). Demarcation refers generally to the ways in which pictorial space is broken up. This list is by no means complete, but it gives you ideas of the options available for creating a visual statement, both formally and personally.

Developing a Style. The aesthetic choices you make, consciously and subconsciously, will determine your style. You begin to find your own style by experimenting with techniques and media, combining them to create special effects (figs. 8-24, 8-25). The best way to attain a personal style is to concentrate on making your illustrations communicate clearly, choosing elements appropriate for each assignment and allowing your expression to emerge from the technique.

Different techniques, media, and approaches appeal to different personalities (figs. 8-26, 8-27). Such factors as the way you use pen-and-ink, whether your brush strokes are tight or loose, your method of cutting a linoleum block, even whether you tear or cut collage elements will set your work apart from that of other artists. The more you draw, the more you strive to communicate through images and symbols, the more your style will develop. Given time and energy, it will become more confident, evolving naturally through your work as a student and as a professional.

Figure 8-22. This soft, realistic illustration of two greyhounds was used to illustrate a book of blank pages. Medium: Pencil. (Illustrator: Laura Hutton)

Figure 8-20. *Pit Bull Editorial*, a student illustration for an editorial assignment. The student chose to juxtapose two violent images, using a drawing style that reflects the drama of the moment. Media: Ink and graphite. (Illustrator: Greg Houston, Pratt Institute)

Figure 8-23. This fashion illustration employs bold, descriptive, calligraphic lines to depict the model and her diaphanous garment. Medium: Charcoal. (Illustrator: Geoffrey Gertz)

Figure 8-24. *Skier*. This airbrushed illustration was created for the 1988 Beef Industry Council winter promotion and was used on posters, banners, and mobiles in grocery stores all over the country. Medium: Gray acrylic. (Illustrator: Elvira Regine; © BIC and Arian & Lowe Advertising)

Figure 8-25. *Skier II*. The same illustration in high-contrast silhouette, created for use in newspapers and coupons. Media: Cut Pantone film on vellum. (Illustrator: Elvira Regine; © BIC and Arian & Lowe Advertising)

Figure 8-27. *Exotic Luxury*, an illustration about duck hunting on the Yucatan peninsula in Mexico from the *New York Times* "Outdoors" column. Medium: Pen-and-ink. (Illustrator: Glenn Wolff)

SUGGESTED PORTFOLIO PROJECTS

1. Create a realistic product illustration for a newspaper advertisement. Product suggestions include athletic shoes, women's handbags, luggage.

2. Create a realistic advertising illustration, emphasizing texture and form, for furniture or glassware.

3. Illustrate three accessories for men (shoes, ties, a wallet) for a retail ad. Make the drawings realistic, but include some symbolic imagery aimed at attracting the business or professional man.

4. Illustrate a house for a real estate advertisement; depict the inviting nature of the neighborhood.

5. For an article on romance in the workplace, create an image or a series of images to convey the attraction of two employees and the conflicts that might arise from their relationship.

6. For an article on home repair, illustrate a house before and after renovation. Give the house human qualities that evoke appropriate emotions.

7. Illustrate an excerpt from a mystery novel. Create atmosphere and tension through facial expressions, body language, and appropriately distorted background details.

8. Use fantasy and humor in an illustration about dieting and the temptations that dieters face.

9. Illustrate a children's story about bringing toys to life. Change and combine the object's physical characteristics by putting them into unnatural contexts, using contrast and exaggeration.

10. Create a holiday illustration, avoiding personal symbolism and cliched imagery.

CHAPTER 9

PROFESSIONAL ISSUES

Illustration for self-promotion used on a business card. Medium: Pen-and-ink. (Illustrator: Kevin Sprouls)

W hether you provide illustrations for textbooks, book covers, magazines, newspapers, record album covers, billboards, or any of a thousand other avenues, when you work as a commercial illustrator, you are not selling original works the way a fine artist does. In today's competitive design climate, five to fifty other illustrators may vie for the same job. In addition to producing quality art, a well-designed and focused portfolio will be the most helpful tool for obtaining work. Beautiful illustrations hidden in drawers will bring neither recognition of your talent nor consideration for assignments. No matter what you specialty is, then, the secret to success lies in building your own reputation.

Although your work should speak for itself, you must satisfy clients' questions about your professionalism. They expect you to be reliable, responsible, and flexible; to meet deadlines; and to create work that adds value to their projects. In return you can expect appreciation for your unique contribution and prompt payment from them.

You can focus your job-hunting effort by deciding whether you would prefer to be a salaried employee or a free-lance illustrator. A salaried employee works in the art or design department of an established company. A technical illustrator might work for an automobile manufacturer, for example; a medical illustrator might be employed by a research-oriented hospital; a general illustrator might be on the staff of a design firm. Most illustrators, however, work in a free-lance capacity, which means that they are in business for themselves, responsible for finding projects and generating income. Whichever route you choose, you will need to develop a portable showcase for your work, a portfolio.

DEVELOPING A PORTFOLIO

The most important thing you will ever do as a professional illustrator is to set up your portfolio. Its contents are critical. Unfortunately, there is no predetermined formula for doing this; however, a successful portfolio should reflect the market, or markets, to which you are selling. Art buyers prefer viewing portfolios with a consistent point of view and type of imagery because it is a reassurance that what is requested can be delivered. A well-structured portfolio may also help you get a job over a more talented illustrator simply because it looks more professional and because it allows an art director or editor to identify your style.

In deciding how to market your talent, you have two choices: either become a "style chameleon," a jack-of-all-trades who can handle any paying assignment, or concentrate on developing a specific style, perhaps following an individual artistic drive. Keep in mind that the most successful illustrators are those who can work in a variety of markets. When work is slow in one market, they take up the slack in another. So organize your portfolio to show a definite style, but do not let it typecast you. Vary the contents of your portfolio from call to call, depending upon what you think particular art buyers will want to see.

General Guidelines. Let's assume you are putting together a general portfolio to present to advertising and editorial markets. What should be included? What should not? As a general rule, your portfolio should contain about three parts commercial pieces to one part experimental work. Your portfolio should include a minimum of ten pieces. An art buyer can usually tell whether you are right for the job by looking at five or six samples, so do not overload your portfolio with too many samples. You should have enough pieces to show your range and style, but do not let the work become repetitive or time consuming to review.

First impressions are powerful, and final impressions are lasting, so begin and end with a strong piece. Assemble all of your work and edit brutally. (The process of editing your work will continue throughout your professional career. And honestly evaluating yourself will make it easier to accept art buyers' criticism.) When you have finished choosing your strongest work, review the examples you have included and remove the weakest piece. These are tough tasks, but they will pay off. A lean portfolio that presents you in the strongest light will serve you better than one overflowing with mediocre work. A note on including published work in your presentation: do not be seduced into showing pieces from prestigious clients that do not display your work to its best advantage.

Assembling Your Portfolio. Present your portfolio samples in a form easy for the art director to handle and examine, either loose or in a ring binder. To reinforce a sense of consistency, place works with related imagery and point of view adjacent to one another. This is especially effective when two pieces are viewed together in an open spread of a ring binder.

Once you have decided on a format, have all of your work reproduced at the same size. Standard reproduction sizes are eight by ten inches, eleven by fourteen inches and fourteen by seventeen inches. The size you choose will be based on three factors: the average size of the original art, the complexity of detail within each piece, and the size of your portfolio case.

Do not include original art. It is often fragile, it may have corrections included as pasted-on patches, and it does not allow the client to see how your work looks when printed. Although reproduced art always varies, for better or for worse, from the original, it will provide a more realistic look at the end results.

You may change methods of reproduction depending on media. For black-and-white line or stipple art, use reproduction-quality photostats. They most nearly approximate what occurs in the commercial reproduction process, where line becomes blacker and light smudges disappear. For work that requires halftone reproduction, such as pencil, airbrush, and watercolor, use a good-quality Velox, continuous-tone photostat, or photographic prints. A Velox breaks the tone down into dots, similar to the effect of a printed image. A continuous-tone photostat resembles a black-and-white photograph in that it shows a range of values from light to dark; however, it may eliminate some subtle details.

A carousel of 35mm slides does not make an effective working portfolio, since your client may not have a slide projector or light box at hand. You should have more than one portfolio, however, and one of the duplicates can be on 35mm slides for easy shipping. Having duplicates will save you from losing jobs because your portfolio is across town. The practice of dropping off a portfolio is widespread, especially in large cities and with agencies, where more than one buyer looks at each collection.

Both your samples and your portfolio case should be in excellent condition. Keep the zipper or latch in working order, and do not let the pages get stuck in the rings of a binder. Label loose samples with your name, address, and phone number, which should also be displayed prominently at the front of the portfolio.

WORK SAMPLES

Art directors frequently ask to receive samples of your work before seeing you in person. These can be as ambitious as your budget allows. Again, black-and-white line work lends itself well to photocopies or photostats. Collage, airbrush, pencil, and watercolor wash appear best in slides or photographs. Tearsheets show the final product, your work in print.

Label everything you send. For photostats, photographs, and tearsheets, use preprinted adhesive labels or make up a stamp with your name, address, and telephone number. Label slides on the front (when you hold the slide up to the light, the image is correct), with your name, size of the original work, the medium, and arrows indicating the top (fig. 9-1).

OTHER PROMOTIONAL MATERIAL

Resumes. In addition to a portfolio and work samples, you need a resume that lists your achievements. Your resume should contain the following information:

- Professional name, address, and phone number.
- Education and scholarships. List only post-high school degrees. You can also list nondegree studies, such as workshops, seminars, and professional classes.
- Employment. List only jobs related to your field. (If you are starting out or returning after a break in your illustration career, you might want to list non-art-related employment to establish your credibility in the workplace.)

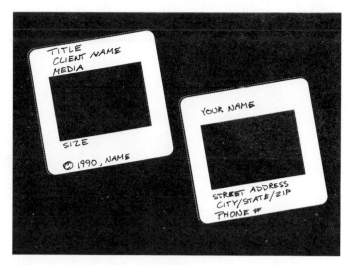

Figure 9-1. Labeling puts all pertinent information at the art director's fingertips, orients the slide for right-side-up viewing, and indicates ownership to prevent loss. The left slide shows the front, the right slide, the back.

- Free-lance assignments. Include a list of clients as soon as possible. Even a small, nonprestigious list of clients will indicate your seriousness of purpose.

- Awards and competitions. List competitions only if you have been accepted or have received an award.

Resumes come in all shapes and sizes. Resume design is often undervalued by otherwise well-prepared job seekers; treat your resume like any important design task. Make sure that all important facts stand out at a glance. Blend form and content in a unique manner. Your ability to organize facts will make a strong impression on employers.

Mailers. A mailer is any printed work you can send to an art buyer to introduce yourself and your style: a single-page information sheet, a postcard, a pamphlet, a booklet, a folder, or a multifold printed piece that accompanies your resume and sample selection (figs. 9-2, 9-3). The work you choose may be reprinted from previous commissions or may be developed specifically for self-promotion. A postcard (printed on lightweight card stock to withstand mailing without an envelope) may hold only one example of your work, along with your name and phone number, if not your address. A brochure that will fit in an eight-and-one-half- by eleven-inch file drawer can display a few examples of your work and include some background information (fig. 9-4).

Leave-behinds. As the name implies, these are items you leave with an art buyer after an interview to provide a reference of your style: individually designed and printed samples, one labeled sample, or an additional copy of your mailer. Be sure that whatever you leave behind will fit into a standard file drawer (fig. 9-5).

Business Cards. A small (two by three and one-half inches) but powerful marketing tool, the business card works like a minibrochure in that it states who you are and what you do. Your business card spreads your name, and perhaps a sample of your artwork, often representing you in the most unlikely settings (figs. 9-6, 9-7).

BUSINESS CONCERNS

As a free-lancer—as your own employer—you take on the tasks of setting up and maintaining a business, including self-promotion, making sales, sending in-

Figure 9-2. One of Glenn Wolff's promotional pieces is this eight-and-one-half- by eleven-inch card that can be included with is mailed promotion or used as a leave-behind sample of his style.

Figure 9-3. This brochure by the Chicago illustrator Elvira Regine reproduces a few of her published spot illustrations. The brochure measures eight and one-half by seventeen inches and is folded in thirds for presentation.

High Wire Act.

The Equinox.

Don't Drink the Water.

Dizzy.

GLENN WOLFF

106½ East Front Street

Traverse City, MI 49684

PHONE: (616) 941-0077

FAX: (616) 941-1177

Park Service Land Grab.

E·L·V·I·R·A R·E·G·I·N·E

ILLUSTRATION & DESIGN • 441 E. ERIE • CHICAGO, IL 60611 • 312•943•7670

Figure 9-4. This postcard mailer was created by the New York illustrator Laura Hutton to promote her pencil illustrations of children.

Figure 9-5. David Street and Renee Gettier-Street operate an illustration studio in Arlington, Virginia. These three promotional pieces show how simply an effective package can be created. Each piece, eight and one-half by eleven inches, shows a single illustration style, using a common layout with a studio logo. The samples are used both as leave-behinds and as mailers.

voices, tracking outstanding fees, and paying taxes. And as the creator of a unique product, you must take responsibility for securing your economic interests and artistic rights.

Become familiar with the contract and copyright laws, and practice your negotiation skills. During initial meetings you and your client should discuss approaches to the illustration assignment, fees, usage rights, and contract terms. Never take a job until you have agreed upon a fee. If you are about to take on a job with a new client, get the fee, deadline, and other pertinent information in writing. A simple letter of agreement or a purchase order can be the key to avoiding potential misunderstandings. Ironing out issues early on will help you avoid loss of economic control and avert legal problems. The difficulties that arise between businesspeople often have to do with an inability to communicate expectations, to describe problems, and to envision solutions.

The basis of a successful partnership between client and illustrator is respect, for ethical practices and for one another. Having a professional attitude means, among other things, being able to explain how you work and helping clients to understand the entire design process.

All of this can seem intimidating to a beginner, but a number of organizations and publications exist to help free-lancers master the mechanics of running a business. The easiest way to keep up with the changes in law and advances in technology, as well as establish contacts, is to join a group. The Graphic Artists Guild, for instance, a national organization of professional artists committed to promoting the economic interests of all artists, maintains branches in major cities. They sponsor workshops and seminars and have published a number of books that deal with the expanding needs of illustrators. You can contact the guild nationally at 11 West 20th Street, New York, New York 10010.

Looking for Work. Whether looking for free-lance assignments or hunting for a full-time job, you may have to visit many potential employers before finding work. Finding potential employers will require some creative searching. The following resources may prove helpful:

- Classified ads: look under Advertising, Art, Graphic artist, and Designer.
- Clubs and organizations, such as art directors' clubs, advertising clubs: ask about lectures and portfolio reviews as well as job listings.

Diane Margolin
Visual Communications
41 Perry Street
New York, New York 10014
212-691-9537

Figure 9-6. This business card for the New York designer and illustrator Diane Margolin provides a witty and effective snapshot of a unique style and technique. The illustration was done on a Macintosh computer.

ANNE WEISZ
Illustration

(416) 782-2604

Figure 9-7. This elegant business card is used by the Canadian illustrator Anne Weisz.

- School career-counseling and job-placement centers: these provide job-hunting information and job listings.

- Yellow Pages: while the Yellow Pages do not list job opportunities, they do list companies that may hire illustrators. Some companies are conveniently classified, including advertising agencies, design studios, book publishers, and so on. Others, not so obvious, include schools, theaters, and manufacturers.

- Publications and directories: every major industry publishes a trade magazine intended to inform the reader of industry news (for example, Advertising Age specializes in the advertising industry). There are also industry directories that list companies by field of activity and subject matter. If you are interested in medical or children's book publishing, for example, the *Literary Market Place* has a complete listing of all the publishers specializing in those areas.

BIBLIOGRAPHY

Doblin, Jay. *Perspective: A New System for Designers.* New York: Whitney Publications, Inc., 1956.

Gosney, Michael, and Linnea Dayton. *Making Art on the Macintosh.* Glenview Illinois: Scott, Foresman and Company, 1989.

Heller, Steven, and Seymour Chwast, ed. *Sourcebook of Visual Ideas.* New York: Van Nostrand Reinhold, 1989.

Hodges, Elaine R. S., ed. *The Guild Handbook of Scientific Illustration.* New York: Van Nostrand Reinhold, 1989.

Hogarth, Burne. *Dynamic Light and Shade.* New York: Watson-Guptill Publications, 1981.

Jennings, Simon, ed. *Advanced Illustration and Design.* Secaucus, New Jersey: Chartwell Books Inc., 1987.

Kerlow, Isaac Victor, and Judson Rosebush. *Computer Graphics for Designers and Artists.* New York: Van Nostrand Reinhold, 1986.

Lozner, Ruth. *Scratchboard for Illustration.* New York: Watson-Guptill Publications, 1990.

Meyer, Susan E., and Martin Avillez. *How to Draw in Pen and Ink.* New York: Macmillan Publishing Company, 1985.

Miller, David. *Dynamic Airbrush.* Cincinnati: North Light Books, 1987.

Morgan, Jacqui. *Watercolor for Illustration.* New York: Watson-Guptill Publications, 1986.

Nicolaides, Kimon. *The Natural Way to Draw.* Boston: Houghton Mifflin Company, 1941.

Oles, Paul Stevenson. *Architectural Illustration: The Value Delineation Process.* New York: Van Nostrand Reinhold, 1979.

Tate, Sharon Lee, and Mona Shafer Edwards. *The Complete Book of Fashion Illustration.* New York: Barnes & Noble Books, 1982.

INDEX TO ILLUSTRATORS

SUBJECT INDEX

OTHER BOOKS FROM DESIGN PRESS

DRAWING AND PAINTING FROM NATURE
by Cathy Johnson
Focusing on pencil, pen and ink, and watercolor, this practical, illustrated volume suggests ways to perceive nature from a fresh perspective and capture those perceptions on paper.
Hardcover $27.45   **Book No. 50002**

SYMBOLS, SIGNS, LETTERS
by Martin Andersch
Elegantly designed, exquisitely produced, and winner of a gold medal at the International Book Art Exhibition (Leipzig, 1989), this collection presents calligraphic art at its finest.
Hardcover $74.00   **Book No. 50006**

HOW TYPOGRAPHY WORKS
by Fernand Baudin
This manual blends handwriting and type to illustrate the nature of individual characters, the assembly of characters into words, words into sentences, and the arrangements of text on a page.
Paperback $14.60   **Book No. 50011**

ARCHITECTURAL DRAWING: OPTIONS FOR DESIGN
by Paul Laseau
This comprehensive study of design communication alternatives for architectural visualization and design brings the many forms of architectural expression into focus and assists readers in the selection of drawing styles for different types of projects.
Paperback $18.60; Hardcover $27.95 Book No. 50008

THE TAO OF CHINESE LANDSCAPE PAINTING: PRINCIPLES AND METHODS
by Wucius Wong
In this beautifully illustrated book, Wucius Wong uses philosophical concepts derived from ancient Taoist and Confucian thought to explain the Chinese landscape painting tradition, its materials, and its brush-and-ink techniques.
Hardcover $29.45   **Book No. 50010**

CALLIGRAPHY TIPS
by Bill Gray
Gray's latest book of tips explores the various styles of hand lettering. Major written alphabets, basic tools, materials, and techniques.
Paperback $12.60   **Book No. 50001**

BOOKS, BOXES, AND PORTFOLIOS
by Franz Zeier
This book is an introduction to the techniques of bookbinding, with instructions for making a variety of boxes, portfolios, book covers, photograph albums, mats, and sewn and adhesive-bound books.
Hardcover $34.45   **Book No. 3483**

BASIC DESIGN: THE DYNAMICS OF VISUAL FORM
by Maurice de Sausmarez
This is a reissue of a classic text with a well-deserved reputation as a clear, authoritative introduction to the basic elements of artistic design.
Paperback $14.60   **Book No. 3631**

3D COMPUTER GRAPHICS: A USER'S GUIDE FOR ARTISTS AND DESIGNERS, SECOND EDITION
by Andrew Glassner
This concise introduction to professional 3D computer graphics techniques gives readers with limited computer backgrounds the information they need to create realistic three-dimensional images, scenes, and animations.
Paperback $26.45   **Book No. 50003**

Look for Design Press Books at your local bookstore or write

Design Press Order Department
TAB BOOKS
Blue Ridge Summit, PA 17294-0850

To order toll-free: 1-800-822-8158

DUE DATE			
SEP 13 '94			
DEC 06 '94			
APR 3 '99			
apr 17			
Nov 3			